A HIGHER CALL TO DUTY

The Unimaginable, True-life Story of

Sgt. Mike McGrew

AS TOLD TO

SARA BUSH

William,
Thank you for all
that you do for Gods
Kingdom and for always
bringing the love and
light of Jesus wherever
you are. May God continue
to bless your hands to
bless others.
Mike McGrew

A HIGHER CALL TO DUTY

The Unimaginable, True-life Story of

Sgt. Mike McGrew

AS TOLD TO

SARA BUSH

A Higher Call to Duty

Cover Photo: Santa Barbara News-Press
Design: Benjamin Cole, David Cole, Michael Bayouth and DP Consulting

Funding for this book provided by the Armand Hammer Foundation

ISBN 978-0-692-13037-7

DEDICATION

Many times, authors will dedicate their books to the people who inspired them. While there are several people worthy in this case, we felt compelled to dedicate our work to God's kingdom. In the process of writing this book, we said a prayer each time we met. It is on our hearts to share it with you:

Dear Heavenly Father,

We dedicate this book to You.
We know that it exists in heaven: a book that will touch many people for Your kingdom.
We ask that You continue to anoint and bless us and let the Holy Spirit author our thoughts, our words, and our actions.
Lord, we thank You for this day and all the wonderful things You are doing in our lives.
We thank You for the opportunity to work on this project and the grace You've poured into our lives as we do, and we ask that You would continue to do so.

In Jesus' name, Amen.

CONTENTS

**While the stories in this book are true accounts from my memory, some of the names have been changed to protect the characters' identities.*

FOREWORD BY
MICHAEL HAMMER

PROVERBS 27:17
As iron sharpens iron, so one person sharpens another.

ROMANS 8:31B
If God is for us, who can be against us?

WE ALL NEED PEOPLE who encourage us in our lives and in our faith and ultimately help us grow closer to the Lord. Sergeant Mike McGrew is one of those people for me. As a man of God, businessman, investor and a philanthropist, I have been involved in many charitable organizations that focus on helping others. I take the time to pray and ask The Lord where He wants me to invest into His kingdom helping others before I commit time and resources to specific charities or embark on any business ventures. 1 John 5:14 states, *"This is the confidence we have in approaching God: that if we ask anything according to his will, he hears us."* I have always been led and honored to support our fine men and women whose service on the front lines in the military, law enforcement, and all around public safety, help us to preserve our country's safety and freedom. I admire and respect their selflessness, their courage and their efforts to help us all live and operate our lives safely and freely while risking their lives on a daily basis to enable us to do so. It was this path that led me to meet Mike following a fundraiser for the local police foundation. At the time, Mike was a board director of the organization, and when he learned about my desire to serve others, he decided to reach out to me to let me know that we had that in common. I invited him to my office to share with me his mission to help law enforcement and veterans struggling with post traumatic stress disorder, addiction, and other deep-rooted issues using a program that God had put on Mike's heart. It was supposed to be a quick meeting. Two hours flew past, and by the end of our conversation, I discovered a genuine friend and confidant in Mike. I quickly saw past his tough exterior, felt his generosity of heart, and I knew that God had a purpose for crossing our paths.

PRODIGAL SON

Because of my position as chairman and CEO of the Armand Hammer Foundation and my physical wealth, people think my life has always been easy. That is just not true. My story is much like that of the prodigal son's in the Bible. I had made some bad decisions as a youth growing up, and my family wasn't pleased. I ventured out on my own and experienced what the world had to offer. I lived for myself, pursuing my own gratification. I lived a life filled with desires of the flesh but realized that these desires could never be quenched as I began to get myself in trouble and hurt myself and those around me. Whether or not I acknowledged Him at the time, God was always present with me and had designed a very different path for me. It didn't take me long to realize that my way of life was empty and leading toward a dead end. It was at my lowest point that God touched me. I had nowhere left to go but up. I did the work I needed to do, went back to my grandfather, Armand Hammer, and asked for his forgiveness. I had to prove to him that I was serious about cleaning up my life, and when I did, he welcomed me back with open arms. It was a valuable, albeit humbling, life lesson, and I understood the mercy of God's love. Just like the prodigal son, I returned knowing that I was being given the invaluable opportunity of a second chance to be with my family.

RICHES GREATER THAN GOLD

They say if you want to see God laugh, tell Him your plans. Mike and I have so many similarities with our rough pasts and living in the world, but we are examples of how God can turn things around. As much as I or Mike tried to put up barriers, it did not matter because God had a plan for both of us. Later in my life, I accepted Christ as my savior and received God's unparalleled grace. Like Mike, I've experienced radical redemption. I know how it feels to accept God's mercy, knowing fully that I don't deserve it. That is so much more valuable than anything on this earth. Like Mike, I want to show others who are at their lowest point that there is hope regardless of what they have done, and there are people who care about them. In his profession as a police sergeant, Mike learned to be the tough guy when he needed to be, but now he is full of compassion. He doesn't judge or condemn others. I admire that about him.

AT EASE

God has given Mike and me a shared vision to support the law enforcement and military community. After that first meeting with Mike, I knew I wanted to join his call to restore the men and women who serve our country. Together, we started the At Ease Program which offers post-traumatic stress counseling and other services to first responders in the region that we reside. The program provides a safe, confidential place and trained, professional people for officers to talk to and, in many cases, pray with. The program continues to make waves with its innovative methods rooted in Christ's love. It is a great privilege helping officers who would not otherwise have the resources offered by At Ease. I have seen the transformative power of the program firsthand, and continue to see God at work. The At Ease program continues to gain momentum and is literally saving peoples' lives.

GOOD AND FAITHFUL SERVANT

I am inspired by Mike's unwavering commitment to growing God's kingdom. He recently traded his badge for a Bible and is now working as a minister. He is often called to speak in front of large crowds, full of men and women from all walks of life. During those events, God often speaks through Mike and his testimony. When Mike decided to put his story down on paper, I knew it would have the ability to touch countless people across the world. I am honored to be a part of his journey, and I pray anyone who reads this book will see God's love through the life of one of his most faithful servants.

FOREWORD BY
PASTOR CHUK REED

WE DON'T ALWAYS KNOW WHY God puts people together. I would have never (never, ever) picked this guy to be a friend! But I guess God is just a practical joker at heart. We are two men from totally different worlds—one from the hood in Los Angeles and one from a classic California beach town—yet in the same place at the same time. I don't know where this will end up, but I know I will never be the same because of my relationship with Sgt. Mike McGrew.

We are two of the most unlikely friends to ever form a bond, yet here we are—brothers in the fire and on fire for the Lord.

I grew up in Watts, California, in the 60s and 70s. I remember the National Guard marching behind armored vehicles during the Watts riots. This was a time when police and community were not the best of friends. It seemed as though the cops didn't like me, and I didn't like them much either. And I was cool with it.

As I grew up, I found myself in church more. The girls were nice to me, and it kept me out of trouble, and trust me, I was always in some kind of trouble. Trouble seemed to follow me around like a shadow. Then one day I fell in love with a smart college girl. By the 80s and 90s, I was married with children. I'd invested into my family, church, and my job, and as the years blew by, my walk with the Lord became deeper, and my calling became a yell!

In 2007, my journey led me to a job as a pastor in a new city, in a whole different cultural environment, a beach town. I was assigned to pastor a small traditional black church in a predominately white populated city. On my first Sunday as pastor in town, I was a little nervous, so I took a little walk about an hour before service just to relax. I found myself walking through the local park, and out of the corner of my eye, I saw two guys hiding by the bushes tying off their arms to shoot up drugs. I was shocked to see something like this just a few hundred yards away from the church. I prayed to God, "Lord, show me a way to help."

After a few months of struggling to resurrect what was a failing church stuck deeply in its rituals and traditions, I was beginning to feel like nothing I was doing was any help. But God was just getting started.

Through what may appear as a series of random events, it was my perception I had been racially profiled, stopped by the police a few times. If you're a black guy from the hood, and you've ever been stopped by the cops, you're afraid of the police. Being pulled over more than one time was more than enough to make me contact the department and call for a meeting with the police chief to discuss the issue of racial profiling by the department.

After becoming what must have been a pain in the side of the police chief, he invited me to attend the Citizen Academy and do a ride-along and to become a chaplain for the department (a job that I would have never thought I would be doing in a million years). But,

I knew the only way to bring about change was to get involved in the community by getting on the inside. It was in that capacity that I was first introduced to Mike. He was just one of the guys, and I really didn't know him well.

Then I got a "call out," one day, that changed the course of my life. I was called to respond to a residence where an officer had lost a family member and was requesting a police chaplain.

At that time, the officer had no idea my only son, Charles Junior, was dying of a cancer-related setback at the time. All he knew was his son was dead, and he needed a chaplain's prayer.

As I arrived on site, I saw a sea of blue (this was long before Blue Lives Matter or Black Lives Matter was trending). I walked into the house and down a long hallway and, finally, into a room where there on the floor lay the body of a young man (T.T. McGrew). His mother and father stood there screaming and yelling out for help, yet never saying a word because of the pain.

After experiencing a supernatural event in that room, I began studying Mike in the aftermath of his son's death, because I knew I, too, would soon lose my son.

Mike drew closer to the Lord and received amazing strength from God that would allow him to be used as an example for me. God used our broken-heartedness to break down any social barriers and preconceptions we may have had of one another.

At my son's funeral, Mike sat right behind me, and my own brother sat a few rows over. Many of my friends and family members that attended the funeral thought I was in trouble with the law "again" and asked me why so many police officers were there, and why was that big white cop "Mike" sitting right behind me with his hand on my shoulder. One friend thought I was serving jail time and was released just for the funeral and all the police officers were there to make sure I didn't try to escape.

Because of our common desire to grow God's kingdom, Mike and I were able to bridge the earthly things that might otherwise divide us. We shared the same spirit, we shared the same truth. We shared the same pain and brokenness, and yet we also shared the same testimony and power. In the midst of our brokenness, we were there for each other along the path to rebuilding our "new normal" without our sons. Through the pain and sorrow, laughter and midnight tears when no one knew, somehow, we made it through to this point. As time went on, Mike and I became more than co-workers or friends. He became my brother.

On September 11th, 2016, we opened a church, where we serve together to advise the kingdom of God with a ministry of spiritual healing, praise, and prayer.

Working with Mike is a lesson in faith. His trust in God is unbelievable. I tell you, no matter what happens in his life, he gives God the glory. From the good, the bad, and the ugly, he gives God the glory because he knows God is moving in every situation for the good of His kingdom. His life is a living testimony of faith. This man has a way of looking at life through his spiritual eyes and not human flesh. As Mike discusses in this book, nothing is impossible with the Lord. You can't make this stuff up. This story is to be continued.

CHAPTER ONE

ROOKIE

JEREMIAH 29:11

For I know the plans I have for you, declares the LORD, *plans to prosper you and not to harm you, plans to give you hope and a future.*

SOME CRIMINALS ARE EASIER TO CATCH THAN OTHERS

Kenny, the armed robber, wasn't the sharpest tool in the shed. Of course, I didn't know that when I heard the call go out for his arrest. He had just held up a shoe store at gunpoint. He'd gotten away in a stolen white jeep with Maryland plates. I happened to be driving in an unmarked unit near the shopping center involved, listening to the description of the getaway car, when I saw it pull out in front of me. Apparently, it was not Kenny's lucky day. I called in for back up and started following him. The black and whites arrived quickly and pulled Kenny over a few blocks away from the scene of his crime. He didn't seem surprised in the slightest to see the officers approaching, and he didn't put up any fight. As we pulled him out of the car, we could see a loaded handgun along with a shoebox full of cash sitting in the passenger seat. After we handcuffed him, we performed what's called an in-field lineup, which involved driving the victim by the suspect to get an I.D. That is when Kenny made his big mistake. I was standing with him when the car rolled by. Kenny saw the woman inside, looked at me, and said, "Yeah, that's her. That's the woman I robbed." I thanked him for making my job easier and placed him under arrest.

Years later I met Barry, the bank robber we caught "green-handed." We got the call of the robbery at a bank on the upper side of town. Barry had escaped with the cash, but the teller had been able to slip a dye pack into the bag. The dye pack exploded and soaked the cash in red ink. As we searched for Barry, we received a tip of a suspicious man at a local laundry mat. The caller reported seeing a man dumping green food dye and piles of money into a washing machine. When we got to the laundry mat, we looked at a surveillance video, and we were able to confirm Barry's identity and tracked him to a sober living facility where he'd been staying. When we showed up to arrest him, he was there, drunk as a skunk, with all of the stolen cash (needless to say, his attempts to reverse the effects of the dye packs didn't work). He confessed to the crime, and we arrested him on the spot. We don't always catch the smart ones, and after 30 years on the police force, I wish I could say all my cases were as simple as Kenny's or Barry's.

Unfortunately, life is just not that black and white, and being a police officer means dealing with some of the most gruesome shades of grey. My personal life hasn't been an exception. In fact, I decided to write this book while sitting in a hospital bed during my battle with stage-three colon cancer. Hearing the doctor read my diagnosis out loud following a routine colonoscopy was a little surreal for me. During a major surgery that followed the diagnosis, I learned that the disease had spread to my lymph nodes, and this put me in the category of a dire 30 to 60 percent survival rate.

As a cop on a police force in Southern California, I'd faced death on a fairly regular basis over the course of the past three decades. But this was different. I couldn't help but wonder if after all the dangerous situations I'd walked away from, it might be cancer that killed me. I agreed to undergo an aggressive treatment plan, which included half a year of debilitating chemotherapy and some long-term side effects that I still continue to work through. I knew I'd have to take a break from my job and that my life was about to drastically change. But I also knew that whatever the purpose for this trial, God would use it for something good. That might sound crazy to some people. It would have sounded crazy to me ten years ago.

I NEVER PLANNED TO BECOME A COP... OR A CHRISTIAN, FOR THAT MATTER.

Ten years ago, I was a decorated cop who'd successfully solved numerous homicide cases and put away countless criminals. Outwardly, I had it together, and I appeared to be able to handle anything. But on the inside, I was a father losing control. My youngest son was fighting a relentless form of bone cancer, and my oldest son was battling a drug addiction. I had been divorced twice, and my own drinking had led me down a dark path of destruction that I am not proud of today. But I've learned that God can take even the worst scenarios and transform them. I am the perfect example of that.

I was born and raised in a mid-sized suburban Southern California city. My dad worked as a firefighter alongside his brother (my uncle Keith), and they moved up the ranks together. By the end of their careers, my dad held the title of Chief and Keith was Assistant Chief of the local City Fire Department. They came from a family line of firefighters or police officers. You could say public safety ran in my blood, but I never planned to become a cop.

Growing up, God was just a vague concept to me. When I was about 12 years old, my best friend Matt's dad was diagnosed with pancreatic cancer. Matt and I had been best buddies since we were toddlers, and we still are 50 years later. His dad had a dynamic personality, and he was larger than life in Matt's and my eyes. Matt loved his dad intensely. During his battle with cancer, a friend led Matt's dad to the Lord. While he had always appeared to be a strong man, he exemplified strength in the months before he succumbed to his disease. After he became a Christian, Matt's dad shared with Matt about Jesus, and Matt and I talked about the Lord a few times. But after his dad died, Matt did not continue to follow the Lord, and I believe he became deeply hurt and angry towards God. While I didn't believe I needed Jesus in a personal way at the time, I never forgot those conversations about how Jesus was working in Matt's family, and I believe they were the first seeds planted in my journey to salvation.

I had a good relationship with my parents. I was a decent student and a good athlete and was always the life of the party. I had a good group of friends. We may have been a little rowdy, but it was all in fun. I felt pretty good about my life, and I believed I had obtained everything good I had on my own merit. I was proud of my accomplishments. I sailed through school and got decent grades, but it was my athletic ability that earned me a college scholarship. I became a national championship wrestler in high school and planned to compete while working on my bachelor's degree at a four-year university. It was the early 1980s, and I was enjoying life.

Towards the end of my first college wrestling season, I was working on my truck, when a fan blade blew off the engine fan and severely injured both of my hands. The injury was so bad that I was unable to return to wrestling. I lost my scholarship and went through a lengthy recovery. When I healed, I began working in construction and going to school at night. Eventually, I quit going to college, thinking I would finish at a later time. I held various construction jobs, and I was working for a painting contractor when I began to think about going into the fire service. As I explored job opportunities at a fire department, a firefighter I knew suggested I look into the police force and encouraged me to apply. The next thing I knew, I was training for duty. It turned out policing came naturally to me. I'd always felt like a protector, and I really liked the idea of keeping people safe. I even earned my first award for valor within the first few months on the job.

'WHICH ONE OF YOU AM I GOING TO KILL FIRST?'

On one of the last days of my field training, an alert went out about a man breaking windows of businesses in the downtown area. My field training officer, Steve, and I happened to be nearby the call, so we were the first to respond.

It was a sunny Sunday afternoon, and the streets were packed with people. When we got to the scene, we spotted the suspect, a tall and scruffy man in his late 40's, frantically swinging a sword dangerously close to the crowds. We parked our squad car in the street to block oncoming traffic and called for backup.

The sword-wielding man was particularly focused on a bicyclist. He repeatedly lunged towards the cyclist, who was using the bike to shield himself, as the suspect swung the sword at him. I noticed several families nearby, and my first thought was, "We have to get this guy away from these people."

I ran over to the offender with my gun drawn and yelled, "Put the weapon down!" As I'd hoped, he turned his attention away from the cyclist and towards me, in the now-blocked and empty lane of traffic on the street. Steve had moved in on one side of the man, and I was on the other, and we both had our guns pointed at him. The man was still holding the sword like he was ready to strike. He had a crazy look in his eyes, and I could see that he really wanted to hurt someone.

He screamed, "Which one of you sons-of-bitches am I going to kill first?" He looked from me to Steve and back again, and then charged towards Steve, who stood at about five-foot-eight—a stark contrast to my six-foot-three frame. Steve took a step back and tripped over a planter on the sidewalk. As he fell, the deranged man took a step towards him and raised the sword over his head. In that instant, it seemed like everything around me stopped. I began to see things in slow motion.

It was up to me to save my partner's life, and I had to decide whether to shoot in order to do it. I remember seeing the consequences of my actions if I pulled the trigger—news headlines reading, "Cop kills guy in front of downtown crowds,"—but I knew I had to do it. I felt my fingers tighten on my department-issued revolver. I saw the hammer of the gun cock back as I pulled the trigger. All the while, I continued to scream for the sword swinger to turn around. Just before the hammer of the gun fell, sending the bullet to the point of no return, he turned towards me. I released the trigger and my breath.

It was the closest I'd ever come to killing someone at that point, and my adrenaline was on overdrive. The sword-swinger was now focused on me as I moved as quickly as I could down the street, to coax him further and further from the onlookers.

By this time, backup had arrived, and I recognized the sound of a cop car barreling towards me. The newly arrived officer driving the squad car decided to use his vehicle to disarm the crazed and life-threatening criminal. The squad car then struck the suspect, and both the man and his sword went flying on impact before landing hard on the asphalt. The blow didn't have the desired effect. The man got back up and quickly grabbed hold of the sword. I tried a different tactic. I sprayed the criminal with mace in an attempt to disorient him, but my plan backfired along with the wind, and the aerated poison drifted into my eyes and lungs.

I coughed and squinted my eyes, but I kept spraying all the while, and he kept swinging the sword. I could barely see or breathe and was grateful that several other officers showed up and joined my efforts with the mace. They'd also blocked off traffic and the crowds.

Now that the surrounding onlookers were at a safe distance from the sword-swinging maniac, the mob mentality began to kick in. People began to chant, "Shoot him! Shoot him!" It was disheartening to hear, and luckily it never came to that. It took several officers and a whole lot of mace, but the man eventually dropped his sword. Officers tackled, cuffed, and put him into a cop car. After his arrest, we learned he'd snorted amyl nitrite, and in his drug-induced psychotic state had smashed the window of a second-hand store and grabbed the sword, which had been on display. We also learned he'd just been released from prison four days prior for, ironically, trying to run down a cop with a car.

It wouldn't be the last time I was called to risk my life on the job. And while it wasn't the scariest or most dangerous of my career, it was the closest I'd come to killing someone. It was also among the many cases that set into motion some bad habits that would lead to the end of my first marriage.

That night, I got home from work, and my then-wife and I went to our friends' house for a barbecue. I tried to recount the day's events to everyone and couldn't quite capture the gravity of the situation. As I retold the story, I remember feeling the adrenaline wear off, and I had to excuse myself so I could go in the bathroom and throw up. I would come to learn how detrimental the intense emotional impacts, which most cops experience often on the job, were to a person.

Months after my run-in with the sword-swinging maniac, I received my first award for valor, for showing restraint and putting myself in harm's way to protect the community on that call. The award's namesake was killed on duty in 1970 while exchanging gunfire with two armed robbery suspects. The award is presented by a local police support organization each year for valor and outstanding performance. I would receive the honor on two other occasions in my career, and the ceremony would later have a great deal of significance to me. But the first time I received the award, I believed I'd earned it, and I was proud of myself. I was blissfully unaware of the evil I would encounter on the job or the personal agony I would have to endure.

CHAPTER TWO
BUILDING BARRIERS

JOB 12:22

He [The LORD] reveals the deep things of darkness and brings utter darkness into the light.

MAJOR CRIMES AND HOMICIDE: THE MOST GRUELING ASSIGNMENTS IN LAW ENFORCEMENT

In those early years as a cop, I had three kids with my first wife. Our daughter, Taryn, came first, and then our oldest son, Matt (named after my best friend). We were only planning to have two children, but then Michael (or T.T. as everyone called him) came along. Of course, after he was born, I couldn't imagine life without him. I couldn't fathom at the time that I would ever need to.

I graduated from patrol work to major crimes and homicide—one of the most grueling assignments in law enforcement. One area we covered included sex crimes. They are often some of the hardest cases to work because, many times, there is little evidence, and it becomes the victim's word against their abuser's. Unfortunately, I have felt at times that the criminal justice system has occasionally failed the victims I worked so hard to help, but that never stopped me from doing the best job I could do. That was especially true when I met Billy.

Billy had been what we call at risk youth since he was a young boy. He'd had several police contacts as a kid and was no stranger to the police department. One day, I received a phone call from the father of a friend I knew. With great pain, the man told me the story of how two of his children had been molested by a priest at a local seminary. He went on to tell me that he knew another young man who had also been molested by the same priest and that this young man was willing to come forward and report the crime. That's when he introduced me to Billy. As I interviewed him, Billy shared the secret that likely catapulted him into his life of troubles and rebellion. He told me the story of how he'd been continually molested by his priest when he was an adolescent. Billy told me when he was left alone with the priest, the man would molest him on numerous occasions.

I realized that Billy was really the victim, and we had to get him justice. Unfortunately, there is a six-year statute of limitations on abuse cases, and in Billy's case, the time to prosecute was nearly up. So we had to work quickly to collect evidence. It was 1992, and the Catholic Church abuse scandal hadn't yet made the news, and so I knew the case would be tough to win. My victim was a "troubled" kid with several prior police contacts, and my suspect was a priest. But, I was able to track down additional victims and their family members. The victims and their families all corroborated each of the victims' stories. The priest's M.O. was the same in each case. One of the victim's parents even had evidence, which included pictures of their child naked, that they had inadvertently obtained from the priest himself.

Despite the disturbing nature of the allegations, through my investigation, I continued to hear testimony that the church was not cooperative and had alienated the victims and their families as they came forward and reported the abuse. In order to maintain the integrity of the case, I had to be careful not to alert the church to my investigation. I was able to track the suspect down through a credit card and found that he was living and working at Mission in Northern California. I'd gathered enough evidence against the priest to get a search warrant and an arrest warrant with a $1,000,000 bail. I drove nearly four hours up to the priest's new home and served the search warrant to the mission's residential property. It was the first time I'd done anything like that. When we got into the priest's room, we found all we would need to get a conviction.

We were able to prosecute, and the suspect later pleaded guilty in the case. But during the investigation, I learned there was a whole community of people who'd suffered through the same thing Billy had—a whole underground network of people who'd been molested by priests. The families of the victims had trusted these priest with their kids.

We identified several more priests, in our city alone, who'd been suspected of abusing children. The majority of them had been moved to different parishes, and all of the cases fell outside the statute of limitations, so they were not prosecutable at that time.

Several years later when I had been promoted to sergeant of the major crimes detail, the law briefly changed to increase the statute of limitations for child molestation. We re-opened the cases and were preparing several search and arrests warrants for the remaining suspects who were located at several different missions. The week the warrants were being prepared, the Supreme Court ruled to reverse the law to increase the time period on the statute of limitations. That meant we were unable to do anything.

Civil lawsuits were subsequently filed, and we were later required to hand the case files over to civil attorneys. They were able to try the cases in civil court, but the majority of offending priests never faced criminal charges.

The silver lining in all of it, for some of the victims, was that the priests were outed. Some priests were defrocked. But in many of those cases, the church simply moved the known pedophiles to places where there were no kids or they put them in the pedophile institutes developed specifically for priests.

To add insult to injury, many families that had come forward told me that they faced repercussions from the church. Most of the victims and their families told me that the church basically responded by excommunicating them. That was probably the biggest tragedy—seeing what happened to the families. The victims and their families' suffering continued long after the abuse was over. For many, like Billy, the anger he felt as a result of the abuse led him into a life of crime. Others resorted to suicide. The case instilled in me a lot of anger towards the church. It wouldn't be until years later that I could separate what happened from my understanding of God and His character.

Unfortunately, the Catholic priest case was not the only time I felt the criminal justice system failed the victims I hoped to help.

I THOUGHT JENNIFER'S DATE RAPE CASE WAS A SLAM DUNK ... I WAS WRONG

We received a call from a woman named Jennifer, who claimed she'd been drugged and raped after a night out downtown. She came down to the station and told me her story. She'd been at a bar and met an art student named Pete who was studying photography. They began a conversation over drinks, and the next thing she remembered was waking up at his house the following morning. She later learned that she had been photographed as she was unconscious and being raped by a man she didn't recognize.

At that time, we'd seen a lot of date rape cases involving a drug called Gamma-hydroxybutyrate or 'GHB.' The rapist could easily slip it into a drink, and after consuming it, the victim became an easy target. I'd seen people under the influence of the drug, and it was not pretty. They would appear beyond intoxicated, lose bodily function, and basically be out of their mind. But what made this drug particularly dangerous is it only stayed in the system for about 8 hours. Typically, by the time the victim came to and realized they might have been drugged, it would be too late to detect the substance through any blood or urine test.

Jennifer assured us she hadn't had that much to drink and believed she had been drugged, but it was too late to detect anything in her blood. However, because she had evidence that someone had seen the photograph, we were able to get a search warrant for Pete's house. He lived with a couple of fellow art students, one of whom appeared in Jennifer's photo.

In the course of our search, we recovered a number of very disturbing photos of the crime. Pete had apparently brought Jennifer back to the home, and he and his roommates took turns raping her. They photographed the entire thing. In one picture, one of the men was on top of Jennifer smiling, while she lay there passed out.

When I saw the pictures, they made me sick inside. I felt an overwhelming sadness for Jennifer, and I remember fighting back tears. I think as a father, it was nearly impossible not to see my own children in the faces of the victims I worked with on a day to day basis.

In addition to the photos, we recovered additional evidence at the house, which confirmed what we'd assumed after listening to Jennifer's side of the story. We were able to arrest each one of the men involved in the rape, and we began working with prosecutors to build the case against them. It seemed to me the case would be a slam dunk, but I was wrong.

When we went into the preliminary hearing, the judge did not believe there was enough evidence to take the case to trial. In fact, he said in one picture, Jennifer appeared like she "could have been enjoying herself." The judge threw the case out. I was disheartened and upset, but I felt even worse for Jennifer. She assured the prosecutor and me that having us believe and support her had been helpful through the process, but I wished I could have gotten her real justice. She later filed a lawsuit against her perpetrators, and the civil attorney used our criminal case to successfully prosecute the rapists. They were convicted and forced to pay monetarily for their crimes, but they never did jail time.

Like so many others, Jennifer's case took something from me. It left its mark on me and changed me ever so slightly. It became another brick in the wall I began to build inside that would keep people out and my emotions locked so tightly inside.

MY COUSIN DAN JOINS THE FORCE

There were very few people who could get through my tough exterior—among them, my cousin Dan. He and I grew up together, but our parents raised us very differently. Dan grew up in a Christian home, immersed in faith from the time he was just ten years old. I, on the other hand, had been raised by very loving parents, but had no religious upbringing and had no desire to change that. Our backgrounds didn't come between us. We found common ground in roughhousing and goofing off. Dan used to come to my house as a kid, and I'd show off my wrestling moves. Somehow he looked up to me. After high school, Dan went away to Bible school in England, but when he returned, I encouraged him to join me on the police force. I helped him with the application process, and he got hired.

Dan and I worked closely together for years, and he was with me for many of the biggest cases I covered, including the incident with Meagan, a crazed woman with a gun. Police responded to Meagan's house after neighbors in her apartment complex reported her creating a disturbance. When the responding officers arrived on scene, she fired a gun at them and retreated back into her home. Dan was on the SWAT team, and I was on the Hostage Negotiation team, and we were both called into the incident. We set up a command post in a nearby apartment and made several attempts to contact Meagan by phone. On the occasions she answered, she only spoke gibberish, and it became apparent she was out of her mind on drugs.

Eventually, a decision was made to shoot tear gas into her apartment to force her out of the home. Most people would do anything to get away from the "CS" tear gas we used, but Megan didn't budge. She continued to suck up the gas for a good 15 minutes. We had to go in. Dan and two other members of the SWAT team had the unfortunate job of confronting Meagan. She still had a strong hold of the weapon when they approached her front door. As she came out of the house, she pointed her gun at the officers. One of the officers fired a non-lethal beanbag gun to subdue her. The beanbag hit her dead in the eye, but she held tight to her weapon. With her good eye, she looked towards Dan and aimed for him. Dan fired back, but this time with a real gun. Meagan went down, and the officers cuffed her. Paramedics got to the scene and loaded Meagan into the ambulance. Because of the officer-involved shooting, investigators had to comb through the crime scene to determine that the shooting was justified. During their search, they were unable to find the beanbag that the first officer had used, but investigators determined the shooting was justified. Meagan survived the shooting and was sent to a mental institution following her recovery. Surprisingly, a few days after the incident, investigators got a call from Meagan's doctor. He asked if we needed the beanbag bullet back. He'd found it lodged in Meagan's eye socket.

Unlike me, Dan had his faith to fall back on when the nature of the job became too much. He credits the

Holy Spirit with keeping his perspective and getting him through the tough times in our careers. He was never a Bible thumper, but if people were interested, he would talk about his relationship with Jesus Christ. He prayed for me a lot over the years, especially during the times I began to unravel. Dan's personal life wasn't all smooth sailing. The second of his three sons was diagnosed with spinal meningitis when he was 4-months-old. The illness almost killed him. After a brain scan, the doctors told Dan and his wife the illness had caused irreparable brain damage and said in the best case scenario, their son wouldn't be "mainstream" until high school. But Dan and his wife prayed and persevered. During that time, we were both working major crimes, which meant long shifts (sometimes 48 hours straight) and frequent calls to come in and work cases. With young kids, it was rough. We became non-existent fathers. But Dan made the difficult decision to step down and go back to patrol work. The decision was not easy. There's a stigma that you couldn't hack it, but to Dan, it didn't matter. He just wanted more time with his kids. Dan and his wife worked with their son through physical therapy, speech therapy, and special education, and miraculously, their son was mainstreamed by 1st grade. By 6th grade, he didn't need any special help. Dan and his wife praised God for healing their son. It was just one of the many miracles I witnessed over the years, but at the time, I wasn't willing to give God the credit. I pointed to cases like the priest molestation to validate my aversion to faith. I was also seeing the underbelly of society on a daily basis, and that didn't help Dan's case. But he never stopped praying for me. I wasn't ready then, but just as Dan didn't abandon me, neither did God. Dan's prayers didn't go unheard. God began revealing His grace to me in the midst of the macabre. Even when covering the most tragic cases, I noticed something good would ultimately result. Sometimes it was a victim discovering a previously unknown inner strength or a family drawing closer to support one another through a dark time. At the time, I couldn't identify it for what it was, but if I looked for it, it was always there.

CHAPTER THREE
REFINER'S FIRE

ISAIAH 48:10

See, I have refined you, though not as silver;
I have tested you in the furnace of affliction.

LOS ANGELES RIOTS: LIKE A SCENE OUT OF A DISASTER MOVIE

The same year the priest abuse case occurred, the LAPD called in law enforcement officers from all over the state to help manage rioting resulting from the Rodney King beating case.

I had gone to school with just a handful of black students who seemed to be well received by our peers, but I had little knowledge of the issues that faced the black community. When I became a cop, I handled a beat that included a bar patronized by a black population. It was located in an area known for high crime and narcotics activity. The crack cocaine epidemic was in full swing in the early1990s, and we frequently had members of Los Angeles-based black gangs delivering drugs to our local dealers. It seemed the only times I was called to the area involved negative circumstances and a lot of arrests. Needless to say, I wasn't well liked by some members of the black community because of my contacts on the streets. Consequently, when our department was called to help during the Los Angeles riots, I had some preconceived notions about the people and neighborhoods we were going to protect.

When the riots broke out, LAPD called in law enforcement officers from all over the state to help. They even flew in the National Guard. When we got the call, we only had moments to prepare to leave. Many of my fellow officers ran over to a J. C. Penney to buy extra underwear, and that was all we took with us. We met at the local Sheriff's Department and loaded up into vans. We then drove to an army base in the L.A. area. When we arrived, there were a group of state prisoners working among the fire crews. The prisoners were in charge of cooking the food. That night, none of the cops would eat anything, in fear of getting a booger sandwich!

We drove over to the city's police station to get our orders, and there were about 50 people flex-cuffed and sitting on the front steps. Flex cuffs are like plastic zip ties used in place of typical hand-cuffs. At that point, cops were just arresting people and dropping them off at the station before heading back out to the streets. The police chief ordered the release of many of the offenders because there was simply no place to hold them. We were told only to arrest people if they shot at us. That wasn't very reassuring. We were assigned to a community on the outskirts of L.A. As we drove there, we saw abandoned cars stopped in the middle of a major freeway and fires everywhere. It looked like a scene out of a disaster movie. It was surreal.

When we pulled off the freeway, people were attaching chains from their cars to the security grates on store windows to rip them off, then breaking the windows and looting. They had no concern about the police presence watching them. I remember hearing gunshots going off around me.

The first day, our unit was ordered to duty in front of a strip mall. That night, we took shifts sleeping in the van, but no one really got much sleep because carloads of gang members would frequently drive by assessing our location, and the sound of gunfire was common. It sounded like war. At times we would be assigned to walk through ghetto projects, and around us, people were shooting at each other in the streets. At one point, a man was shot and killed just one block away from my location. It was chaos. I remember arguing with people who were burglarizing stores right in front of us. We would yell, "Put that TV back!" And they would simply respond with foul language and say, "Everyone else is doing it!' Other people were just walking down the street with gas cans lighting things on fire. The fire departments were working non-stop all day and night. For many people, there were no apparent consequences. But when the sun rose in the morning, the crime died down, and members of the community would come out. The people would come to us and thank us for being there. They looked us straight in the eye and told us how much they appreciated us saving their city. They were the kindest, nicest people. It was really heartwarming to see, and it made me realize they were the reason I was risking my life. By noon, most people would go back inside. By two in the afternoon, things would start heating up again. The insanity went on for about 5 days.

We got very little sleep, and it was extremely stressful, but the ordeal was also quite eye-opening and taught me a lot about communities. It impacted me and changed my whole perspective. I left L.A. a changed man. Looking back, I see my work during the L.A. riots was part of God's plan to show me His grace and the hearts of the loving people who lived in this community. God was stripping away my judgment and preconceptions about people. I carried that lesson with me throughout the remainder of my career.

More than two decades after my experience in L.A., I was involved in another near-riot situation in my own city, but the results were drastically different, and I give glory to God for that. But at this point in my life, I did not know the Lord, nor did I recognize the lessons He was teaching me along the way.

"HE'S CRAZY, AND HE'S GOING TO KILL HER!"

God began to open my heart for people in a way it hadn't been before. I began empathizing with members of my community that I might not have felt compelled to before, including Chrissy, a crack addict and prostitute that I'd arrested on numerous occasions. In this case, we received a call from a man who claimed his brother, Gus, had gotten in a fight with Chrissy and was planning to kill her. Gus had a gun, and he and a friend were out looking for her. "He's crazy, and he's going to kill her!" Gus' brother warned us. It was late at night in the middle of a graveyard shift. My partner and I were able to locate Chrissy in an apartment building where she was staying. We parked in the back of the building so the cop car wouldn't alert the suspects we were there.

The apartment was on the second floor. It was one of two apartments separated by a small landing at the top of the staircase. We knocked on Chrissy's door, and she welcomed us in. She told us she was aware Gus was upset with her and knew that he would likely kill her if he got the chance. She also told us that she had heard that Gus was on his way to her apartment at that time. We stayed with her inside the apartment, and as we were talking to her, we heard a knock at the door. I answered. The guy standing on the other side took one look at me in full uniform, and his eyes got as big as saucers. He called down to Gus, who was walking behind him just a few feet away on the stairs, "Cops!" As he began to turn to run, I reached out and grabbed hold of his shirt collar and shoved him into the doorway across the landing. That's when I looked down and saw Gus a few feet away from me reaching for a gun he had visibly tucked into the front of his waistband. I immediately reached for my gun. Somehow, I grabbed mine first and pointed it at Gus, all the while still holding his buddy down with the other hand. Gus saw that I'd beat him to the draw, took his hand off his gun, and, while raising both of his hands up, and through a sinister smile, said calmly, "You win." My partner carefully stepped down a few stairs and cuffed Gus as I held him at gunpoint. We arrested both men. Chrissy cried as she realized we had literally just stepped in front of a bullet for her and thanked us for saving her life.

As cops, we put ourselves in harm's way to protect everyone in our community on a fairly regular basis. After some time in the profession, it becomes easy for police officers to begin to believe there are only "good guys" (the cops) and "bad guys" (the crooks or criminals they encounter on a daily basis), and nothing in between. But that is a dangerous way to think. The best thing we can do as cops is make a sincere effort to be part of the community—so we can be stripped of those dangerous notions. There is a big payoff in that because it allows us to see people and allows people to see us for who we really are. When I see the events unfolding across the country right now, I see the importance of law enforcement engaging in partnerships with their community so that everyone has a better understanding of each other when a crisis hits. I know that with all the negative media attention law enforcement officers receive, many people are wary of the men and women in the field. But, the majority of police officers I know are willing to and do risk their lives to protect people they've never met or will never know. I have witnessed it time and time again.

CHUK CONFRONTS THE POLICE CHIEF

Our department wasn't perfect. We dealt with our share of conflicts involving race. One instance concerned a man named Chuk Reed. Chuk grew up in a rough, predominantly black neighborhood in Southern California. He lived a hard life until he found the Lord. He'd been transformed after accepting a relationship with Jesus Christ and that ultimately brought him to my city to pastor a church. Within the first few months of his arrival, he was pulled over four times. He was sure he'd been targeted for the color of his skin, and needless to say, he wasn't particularly pleased with the local police department. He decided to make a formal complaint about racial profiling. He showed up to the department to speak to the then-police chief. He brought other black pastors along with him. The conversation quickly turned in an unexpected direction. The chief asked Chuk if he'd ever considered becoming a chaplain and offered him the position. Like me, Chuk had no intention of working in law enforcement, but after some thought, he accepted the job. I met Chuk shortly after he was hired onto the force, but I had no idea then the impact he would have on my life or that we would one day become closer than brothers.

CHAPTER FOUR

T.T.'S DIAGNOSIS

PSALM 34:18

The LORD is close to the brokenhearted and saves those who are crushed in spirit.

NOTHING TOOK THE PAIN AWAY: I WAS SELF-DESTRUCTING

As the 1990s came to a close, I continued to work my way up the ranks in my department, but things were not going so well at home. My first wife and I divorced, and I was chasing the things the world has to offer for comfort to escape from the tragedies I dealt with at work. I used alcohol and other unhealthy behaviors to take my mind off my life's troubles and trials, but nothing I did took away the pain or trauma. The more I chased alcohol's relief and fleshly desires, the more destruction I caused to myself and those around me. My own parents divorced when I was 30, and it broke my heart. It crushed me to do the same thing to my kids. My downward spiraling attempts to cope, coupled with my hectic work schedule, took a toll on my second attempt at marriage. It would get darker still before I'd see any light at the end of the tunnel.

By 2003, the Iraq war started, but it didn't hit close to home until several months in when I received a call from a lieutenant in the U.S. Army who needed help locating the family of a soldier killed in action. He explained that he was responsible for delivering the death notification, something he had never done before. At that time, I would rather be assigned to any other type of call. I did not like delivering the earth-shattering, life-changing news. (Once I became a Christian, however, these calls took on a very different meaning for me.)

When the lieutenant and I met, he appeared so nervous that I offered to go with him. We located the boy's mother in a nearby town, and on the way to her house, I relayed to the lieutenant what I usually say to the parents and how I typically handled these very delicate situations. My years of experience have taught me that the best way to deliver bad news, especially death notifications, is to be matter-of-fact, yet loving and sensitive, and that loved ones often want as many details as possible. Usually family members have a pretty good idea why we are there when they see the uniforms at the door. We knocked, and the young man's mother answered. When we explained that her 19-year-old son had died when a roadside bomb exploded next to his convoy on a road in Iraq, she collapsed to the floor. As I listened to the lieutenant offer the grief-stricken woman words of comfort, I was struck by how awful the situation really was, not just for the mother and her family, but for the young lieutenant. In the months to come, he would likely be telling other mothers that their child was never coming home, and that job would not get any easier. I knew that better than most. Being with him that day brought the war home, gave it a face and made it personal to me.

MY WORLD UPSIDE DOWN; MY SON T.T HAD OSTEOSARCOMA—BONE CANCER

For as often as I'd had to deliver bad news, I wasn't prepared to be on the receiving end. While battling the cancer that hit me has been brutal, it doesn't compare to watching my youngest son in the fight of his life. Hearing doctors describe T.T.'s diagnosis for the first time was worse than anything I'd experienced in my life to that point. T.T. was just 12 years old and in junior high at the time. He'd started complaining about a pain in his leg a few months before. His mother took him to the doctor on three different occasions, and each time the doctor said the same thing:

"It's growing pains," or "Maybe he just moved his knee the wrong way and twisted it."

But no one really thought anything was wrong. A few weeks later, I took T.T. on a day-long pheasant hunt (a trip hosted by the California Department of Fish and Wildlife), and I noticed he was really limping. The next morning after the trip, he woke up crying at his mother's house.

"My leg is really hurting," he sobbed.

She took him back to the doctor, and this time they did an x-ray. The scan revealed a tumor in T.T.'s knee. The doctors told us it was serious and sent us to Los Angeles the same day for more specialized testing. We were seated in a waiting room at the UCLA medical center next to kids with no hair and missing limbs, and I thought to myself, "Are we going to be one of those families?"

The doctors said they would do a biopsy on the tumor to find out what it was. When the results came back, they informed us, "It's osteosarcoma—bone cancer."

When I heard the words, I just shut down. Doctors told us our best shot of getting rid of the cancer would involve amputating T.T.'s leg from the knee down. We talked to T.T. about his options and ultimately made one of the toughest decisions I'd ever had to make, to go ahead with the surgery.

Prior to the procedure, T.T. had to undergo an intense round of chemotherapy to determine whether the cancer would respond to treatment. We spent 200 days in the hospital the first year T.T. got sick. His treatments lasted five days at a time, and the side effects from the chemo were so bad, he was often too ill to leave the hospital. TT's cancer diagnosis turned my world upside down, and I still can't imagine what it must have been like for him.

In my work life, I dealt with crisis nearly every day. At this point, I knew how to be strong for people around me. I thought I could be that rock for my family, and for a long time, I tried. But T.T.'s diagnosis was like a nightmare I couldn't escape. Every day I'd wake up and think, "He's going to be cured."

But he wasn't.

T.T. became close friends with several of the other kids in the cancer ward. At the same time, I befriended other parents who, like me, were helpless bystanders in the whole process. I remember sitting in the hospital and looking over to see another dad who had the same look on his face as I did on the first day of T.T.'s diagnosis. I knew his life had just been turned upside down and that he was scared and unsure and shaken. I walked up to him and introduced myself and tried to offer my support. But at the time, I was trying to figure it all out myself. Even before T.T's diagnosis, he was known as the kindest and the gentlest kid. Everybody loved him. Maybe that's why it seemed so unfair that he would receive this likely death sentence when his life was really just beginning. He fought hard, but the cancer was relentless.

When people would talk to me about God and tell me He offered peace, I wanted nothing to do with it, and sometimes I'd get really angry. I believed there was a God, but I'd watch my son suffer, and all I could think was, "Why would He allow this to happen?"

Despite my feelings, I attempted to put on a brave face. I felt like I had to because I was often in the public eye. I always tried to look for the good in a bad situation. Much of the time, it wasn't too hard to find. The people I worked with were incredible in their support of T.T. For example, local law enforcement and emergency agencies offered our family a lot of support during that tough period. The police and fire departments held a fundraiser barbecue to help cover the costs of T.T.'s medical care. They sold chicken sandwiches for about $7. Incredibly, about 10,000 people showed up, and raised enough money to pay for years of T.T.'s expensive treatments.

THE HUNT OF A LIFETIME

Four years after TT's diagnosis, he was given a rare opportunity to hunt grizzlies in Alaska through a program called "Hunt of a Lifetime." It's sort of like the Make-a-Wish program but with firearms. Through the organization, T.T. had the opportunity to choose where and what to hunt. The idea didn't seem all that unconventional because T.T. and I had spent a lot of time hunting and fishing together before he got sick. When he learned he'd been chosen to get his wish, I asked him, "Would you want to go somewhere to hunt elk?"

"I was thinking brown bears in Alaska," was his response.

As usual, he wasn't just thinking of himself. He knew I'd always wanted to go to Alaska, and I think he chose the trip for me.

I asked, "Are you sure?"

"Yeah," he said.

I envisioned something a little less dangerous (Alaskan brown bears are among the largest breed of grizzly), but I underestimated my son.

We took the 10-day trip in October of 2007. It took two separate flights in small bush planes to get to the remote village located in the Aleutian Islands. The landing strip was literally just a stretch of dirt. There were about 140 Native Americans who lived in the village, including the man who would guide us through some of the most rugged terrain I'd ever traversed. We slept in a weathered and worn-out hut, but it was wonderful because it was heated during the freezing and harsh weather.

T.T. was one of three kids to go on this particular Hunt of a Lifetime, but each kid got his own guide. Our guide had grown up in the village and knew the land like the back of his hand, down to every trail.

The first day, we took ATVs out and headed for the

top of a mountain where we would scan the countryside with binoculars and a spotting scope, searching for bears that could be seen a few miles away. When we spotted a bear, we would take the ATVs down to the marsh area and then once we got within a mile of a bear, we left the ATVs and hiked.

The excursion was not only dangerous, it required navigating through thick brush, dense marshes and rushing rivers, and all in extreme weather—conditions that would be difficult even for people with no physical disadvantages. T.T. had had his leg amputated through the knee when he was first diagnosed with cancer and had to use a prosthetic leg. When we had to cross the rivers or marshes, I held T.T.'s rifle, and he hung on to me as we hopped through the water together. It wasn't easy, but T.T. did it without complaint.

On the first day of the hunt, we spotted a bear and went into the river area and began stalking it. The guide was tracking the bear tracks, which were very large and fresh. He told us that judging by the size of the tracks, this bear was a ten-foot square bear, which they measure from the length of the tail to the head and from the distance between its front paws when stretched out. This meant that the bear we were stalking could have bee up to thirteen feet tall when it stood on its hind legs. As we followed the tracks, the guide noticed that the bear was circling around us and was most likely stalking us. The guide then told us, "We need to leave the area right now. This bear is too old and smart and is hunting us!" We left the area and returned to our spotting location.

At the top of the mountain we used for spotting, the views were stunning—on one side the Pacific Ocean with several marshes and rivers running into it, and on the other side you could see volcanoes and mountain ridges covered in snow. While beautiful, it was also freezing up there. Surviving the environment was a test in itself. We would be hugging bushes to hide from the gusting winds, snow, and at times, wet slush. T.T. was pretty tall for his age. At 16, he stood about five-feet, eight-inches tall. It was funny to see him attempt to squeeze his large frame under a little fort he made out of branches as he tried to hide from the elements. But T.T. always had a good sense of humor about things. He was able to laugh at himself. After he first got his prosthetic leg, he had to get used to the rhythm of swinging his leg for each step, and he fell down a lot. But instead of getting mad, he made jokes about it.

It was no different on this hunt, and we had to find ways to pass the time. We spent a lot of time sitting and waiting as we searched for small specks below us that could potentially be our targets. So we had hours to talk and get to know our guide and each other better. One thing we all had in common was wrestling. The guide had been the Alaskan State wrestling champion. T.T. and I had both wrestled on the high school team. I had also gone on to wrestle in college (something my son would never get a chance to do).

Luckily, our guide not only knew the land, he knew the animals well, too. Because it was October, the bears were at their biggest. In the spring, they are just coming out of hibernation and are skinny, but in the fall, they're getting ready to go back to sleep, and they're really stout. On the fourth day of our hunt, we spotted a grizzly.

We always had to be aware of which way the

winds were blowing. Bears have such a keen sense of smell; if they caught our scent, they might run away, or worse, begin hunting us. The alder trees in the terrain were so thick it was nearly impossible to see, let alone walk through them. Of course, the bears could get through with no problem. We were looking across a river towards a grass valley where we had spotted a bear from the mountaintop when I heard these two crunching sounds behind me, and I felt the ground shake under my feet. I looked at the guide and said, "I think the bear is right behind us," and he said, "Yeah. I think so."

We hiked along this narrow riverbank in thick brush taller than us. The guide thought he saw the bear in some trees, and he told me to go stand a few feet away while he stayed with T.T. I stood in this place where the river bends, so I couldn't see anything more than twenty yards in front of me, and pretty soon I heard the guide snapping his fingers at me. He said, "I see the bear just ahead."

So we walked up the river and reached a small island where we waited and waited, and the next thing I knew, the guide saw the bear out of the corner of his eye. It had gone around us! It stood up, and I could see it was huge! The grizzly dropped back down on all fours and lumbered towards us. I yelled at T.T.

"Take a shot!"

He did, and he hit the bear. But instead of stopping it, the bullet just made the bear angry, and it continued towards us.

I ran towards the bear, and the guide ran towards the bear. We both shot at the bear as we ran. I don't remember how many shots we fired. But I do know that T.T. fired the fatal shot. The grizzly died about twelve feet away from us on the last shot. It was one of the most intense experiences we shared together.

During our trip while waiting for our plane in the airport, I met an army captain who'd lost both legs in a parachuting incident. He was traveling as a motivational speaker. I called T.T. over and said, "Hey, show this guy your leg!" T.T. lifted his pant leg and revealed his prosthetic. The two were instantly buddies and bonded over their stories of survival and perseverance.

T.T. and I were already close heading into that hunting trip. That's what happens when a person has cancer, it gives you time to say the things you need to say, unlike parents who lose their children in a car crash or other freak accident, who don't realize they are spending the last minutes with their kids. As a police officer, I already understood the importance of telling people around me how I felt about them. I'd seen how quickly life can be taken away and how families can be ripped apart without a moment's warning. I never walked away, hung up a phone, or went to bed without telling the people I care about most, "I love you."

Still, this trip brought us closer together. We had a chance to strengthen our father-son bond. When T.T. died, I knew we'd said all we needed to say to each other. Now I can see our experience in Alaska was a gift from God, even if I wasn't aware of it at the time. T.T. lived a couple more years after the near bear attack and continued treatment for his disease, but ultimately, it wasn't the cancer that killed him.

CHAPTER FIVE

WAR ON DRUGS

1 JOHN 2:16

For everything in the world—the lust of the flesh, the lust of the eyes, and the pride of life—comes not from the Father but from the world.

DESPITE WORKING NARCOTICS, I FAILED TO NOTICE MY SON'S STRUGGLE

T.T.'s diagnosis had a huge impact on the whole family, including his older brother, Matt. Watching someone you love battle cancer can be tougher than being in the fight yourself. With T.T., there was nothing I could do to save him from the disease. And when my oldest son Matt's struggle with drug addiction began, it was excruciating to watch and to realize I was also powerless to free him.

Matt had always been a person with an enormous and caring heart. He always put the needs of others before his own as a kid and as an adult (during times of sobriety). He was a loving child filled with laughter and often put himself in the role of a peacekeeper in our family and during any type of conflict between others. Even as a child, he did what he could to smooth things out and make everyone around him happy. I believe that because Matt cared for others so much, his pain was enormous when he saw his brother T.T. suffer. I'm sure Matt witnessed how I used alcohol to self-soothe and cope with my own inner struggles, and that may have made it easier for him to do the same. I don't make excuses for bad choices, but it makes sense that once the door to drugs was opened, Matt tried to cope with his emotions by not feeling at all.

Matt began using drugs when he was about 15 years old. He started smoking pot on occasion but soon graduated to harder drugs. People ask me whether I knew what was going on right away, but the truth is, I didn't (or I didn't want to see it).

I'd worked a lot of narcotics enforcement and could spot a drug deal a mile away, but when my own son was using right under my nose, I was blind. When things would get fishy, I'd give him the benefit of the doubt, but the signs were there. His grades started slipping. He started telling me lies, and once the drugs really took hold of him, I could read it all over his face. His complexion changed, and he lost a lot of weight. His addiction would eventually spiral out of control. Until then, the only war on drugs I focused on involved the dealers and users I faced while on patrol.

UNDERCOVER STING; "IF YOU'RE A COP, I'M GOING TO SHOOT YOU RIGHT NOW"

While I was working in the narcotics unit on a

temporary assignment, we were tracking a known drug dealer in town named Sam. The detective in charge of the case had set up an undercover cop from another area to make a significant drug deal with Sam. They were supposed to meet in a parking lot to the rear of a strip mall. Sam's brother, Johnny, showed up to negotiate the deal. Johnny was a dealer and a user, and he was paranoid and unstable because of his drug use. The undercover cop was wearing a wire during the negotiation, and I was sitting in an unmarked car nearby, along with a DEA agent, listening to the conversation. During their exchange, Johnny pulled a gun on the undercover officer and yelled, "You better not be a cop! If you're a cop, I'm going to shoot you right now!"

We were prepared to step in, but the undercover cop stayed cool and handled the situation really well. He was able to talk Johnny down and negotiate the deal for the next day. The plan was to execute what's called a flash (someone flashes the money and the other flashes the dope) before the trade. The morning of the sting, we were ready. We put two snipers on top of the strip mall overlooking the parking lot in which the deal would go down. There was a team assigned to make the arrests, a team assigned to track the money, and a team assigned to protect the undercover officer (often when the cops show up, the crooks will go after the undercover guy).

It just so happened the local Sheriff's Narcotics Team had recently obtained a new van. They agreed to lend it to our department with a warning, "Whatever you do, don't screw up our new van!"

I was assigned to the arrest team. We were staged in the back of the van. We had DEA agents, sheriff's deputies, machine guns and everything you could think of in this van. We were parked in the front of the strip mall, waiting for the signal. The flash went down smoothly, and we got the go-ahead to make the arrests. But just as we were moving in, the dealers got spooked and decided to split. They were in their own oversized van. They attempted to escape through the parking lot as we began chasing them. That's when the sergeant from our Department yelled to our driver to "Ram them! Ram them!"

The driver did. We rammed into the criminal's van while traveling at about 25 miles per hour. We disabled the criminal's van but destroyed the Sheriff's Narcotics van in the process. We were able to pull the guys out and arrest them, and we found enough evidence to convict the crooks, which included a large amount of cocaine. Johnny went to jail for the crime, but he was released years later.

It didn't take him long on the outside before he committed another crime. He was being pursued by California Highway Patrol officers and was speeding through town when he slammed into another car, killing the driver. When our agency was dispatched to the scene, a fellow officer and good friend, Eric, arrived first. He immediately recognized the victim's vehicle. It was his brother's car.

I knew I wasn't the only officer on the force to experience tragedy outside of the job. Eric was a Christian, and watching how his faith played out in the midst of losing his brother in such a senseless way was moving. It impacted me and chipped away another small piece of that wall I'd been working on for years. Much of the time, I could ignore the voice in my head questioning the real meaning in all of it. The physical nature of the job certainly helped to quell any real soul-searching.

"THIS GUY IS CRAZY! HE'S NUTS! HE'S LIKE NOTHING YOU'VE EVER SEEN!"

I may not have lived out my wrestling career as I'd liked, but my wrestling skills came in handy on several occasions when I had to take down a criminal like heroin dealer Hector, who wanted to put up a fight.

Hector had been on our radar for quite a while. Two of our undercover officers were conducting surveillance for an unrelated case when they spotted Hector on the street doing his own illicit business. They decided to confront him. They got out of the unmarked car and walked over to Hector. When they got close enough to him, they identified themselves as police officers and ordered him to stay put. But their attempt to arrest him didn't go as planned. Hector fought back—hard. During the fight, he inflicted injuries on the officers. At one point in the struggle, Hector grabbed hold of one to the officers' gun, but the officer did not lose control of the weapon. He then managed to escape over an eight-foot fence nearby. When the officers returned to the station, they had to do a little walk of shame. We had to give them a hard time for letting the bad guy get away, despite the fact that they outnumbered him. I was among those razzing the two undercover officers, but they maintained that Hector was tougher than your average criminal.

"You guys don't understand," one of the officers said, "This guy is crazy! He's nuts! He's like nothing you've ever seen!"

I just laughed and told them I had met Hector

in the past, and I didn't think he was anything out of the ordinary. I'd had my own run-in with him just a few weeks prior during a raid at a "drug house." We were able to do a body search, and when we found his drugs, he put up a struggle, but we had no problem subduing him and getting him into custody. We continued to tease the officers for several days until an informant gave us information that Hector was staying in a motel in a nearby town. We didn't have time to get a warrant, so we decided to use a common police tactic—knock on the front door loudly and identify ourselves as the police. In most cases, that's enough to scare a criminal out the back door or window, and we have officers waiting for them outside. Once they are outside, we don't need a warrant to make the arrest.

We assembled a team to go pick up Hector. It included a few cops, my partner and me, and the two undercover officers who had something to prove. When we got to the motel, my partner and I agreed to take the back window. We knew we could handle Hector, and we figured we could show the other guys how it's done. The two undercover officers knocked on the motel room door, and sure enough, we heard the back window crank open. As soon as Hector hopped out onto the window ledge, we grabbed him and pulled him down. He hit the ground hard, and I thought for sure we had him. But he just jumped right back up, and the battle began.

He started punching me in the face and punching my partner. He somehow managed to ram my head into the window. The window cut my forehead open. My partner also got his head split open during the fight. At one point, I looked up and saw the undercover cops watching, and after the fight was over, I'm pretty sure I saw them smiling. We did eventually get Hector into handcuffs, but my partner, another detective, and I ended up in the hospital for stitches. It turned out Hector really wasn't someone you wanted to fight. Dealing with people on drugs often leads to dangerous circumstances, and some cases don't end as well as Hector's.

"I KILLED A MAN. WHAT CAN I TELL MY CHILDREN?"

We got a call from a father whose adult son was freaking out on meth. The young man had been living in a storage shed in his dad's backyard. The father had reached his wit's end with his son's addiction, but he wasn't quite ready to give up on him and kick him out (the area between the rock and the hard place I knew all too well).

During a particularly violent episode on the drug, the son wrote bizarre messages on the walls of his makeshift shelter before attempting to light the shed on fire. That is when his dad decided to call us. When officers arrived, the young man was standing in the front yard with the knife in his hand. Officers tried to talk the man down from his drug-induced rage and convince him to drop his knife, but the man refused to comply. The suspect ran into the housing complex armed with the knife, and the officers chased him into a small backyard area behind his father's housing complex. The suspect and the officers were now cornered in a confined space. That's when the man held the knife up and charged towards an officer named John. This incident happened a short time before tasers became standard issue within most police departments. John had no choice but to shoot the man, killing him instantly.

At that time, I was working as the Homicide Sergeant, so I was called to the scene to investigate. One of the first things I noticed was how visibly shaken the officer appeared. As we were wrapping up the investigation, John came to me and asked me, "How can I even go home and face my family after this? I killed a man. That is not what I am supposed to do. I am supposed to be helping people. What can I tell my children?"

As cops, we often go into situations knowing that the use of deadly force may be required someday, but for the most part, I think almost all cops never want it to come to that. We do everything we can to keep that from happening. While I have been present at and have investigated a number of officer-involved shootings, I have never had to use deadly force. I have come close on several occasions. I believe training is key in keeping your head and making the right decisions in life-and-death situations. I also credit the Holy Spirit for giving me discernment. I am not alone. I work with men and women of courage and character. We're always looking for the peaceful way out. Unfortunately, sometimes that isn't possible. Unfortunately, too many members of the public have lost their trust in law enforcement because of nationally publicized use of force issues or, at times, sensationalized incidents involving law enforcement which do not accurately show the entirety of events which lead to a use of force. Cops are in harm's way every day. For every officer-involved shooting, there are multitudes of cases where an officer could have shot a suspect but didn't. Unfortunately, the media doesn't often focus on those scenarios.

These days we read a lot about things that don't go well for police officers, but you don't always see the many good things that happen every day that officers are doing out on the street to protect our communities.

The incident with the meth addict would haunt John for years. Luckily, God had a plan to heal him, but that part of the story would not occur until about a decade later.

The investigation also brought up a lot of emotions for me because I couldn't help but put myself in that father's place when I looked at the young man whose life had been cut tragically short, ultimately as a result of his battle with drugs. I knew I could be facing a similar situation someday.

When people are under the influence of drugs and alcohol, they are not themselves. The poison possesses them. It becomes like an impenetrable prison they cannot escape. It is nearly just as impossible to break through from the outside. I eventually accepted that my son Matt had a problem and tried everything in my power to help him in his struggle to break free of the cycle of drug use. I tried tough love. I tried holding his hand through the process. Nothing seemed to work long-term. There were times I blamed myself for his actions. I went through the roller coaster of emotions that those with loved ones who struggle with addiction go on. Each time my son would relapse, my heart would break. But as much as I would be disappointed and frustrated, I never stopped loving him with the intense love of a father for his son. This simple fact would have a profound impact on me later. It would help me to grasp the extent of God's love for me.

CHAPTER SIX
187

EPHESIANS 6:12

For our struggle is not against flesh and blood, but against the rulers, against the authorities, against the powers of this dark world and against the spiritual forces of evil in the heavenly realms.

COLD CASE; INTRODUCTION TO THE SUPERNATURAL

In all my years on the force, just one of my homicide cases went cold—the murder of Frank. It was a Sunday in 1995. The call came in the late night hours. A man's body had been discovered in the parking lot of a local music amphitheater. The victim had been brutally murdered in the middle of the night, and I was assigned to the investigation.

We immediately began processing the crime scene and collecting evidence, but protocol required us to wait for the coroner to arrive to check the man's ID. He was dressed nicely with a button-down shirt. In the breast pocket of his suit, we found a prayer card (a small piece of paper with a picture and the words of a prayer printed on them, often given out by the Catholic Church).

We could tell there was handwriting on the back of the card, but due to the amount of blood soaked into the devotional, we couldn't tell what it said. We sent it to the crime lab in hopes they might be able to make it out.

The victim's blood-soaked clothes also left some clues about the moments leading up to his death. We could tell his physical positioning when he died and other details about his actions prior to death. A few hours after I'd arrived, the coroner showed up and pulled the man's wallet from his pocket. That's when we learned our victim's identity: He was the brother of one of our fellow police officers.

Before pursuing any leads on the case, I had to notify Frank's family of his death. His brother took the news extremely hard.

It was weeks before we got our first real lead into Frank's murder. The crime lab had been able to piece together the message written on the back of that prayer card we found. It included a name, followed by a San Diego County phone number, and the name of a local grocery store that had been closed for several years.

My partner and I immediately got in the car and headed south to have a chat with the person whose name was written on the card. We arrived at his home and knocked on the door. When he opened it, we identified ourselves as detectives, and he immediately asked, "You're here about Frank, aren't you?"
We said, "Yes," and I immediately thought, "This may be our guy."

I figured at the very least, he knew something

about Frank's death. He invited us in and told us he'd worked with Frank 10 years before at the grocery store named on the prayer card. He said he'd had a dream the night before Frank's murder.

"In the dream, Frank was being attacked," the man told us.

The man went on to describe Frank's physical actions (which were consistent with the evidence we found) and the scene, including landmarks which were at the crime scene. He described the crime scene perfectly. He also mentioned the prayer card. Although he said he didn't know what any of it meant, he said he woke up the next morning and felt the need to call Frank to see if he was okay. He said he'd tracked down Frank's dad's number and called him. He left a message with Frank's dad, including his name and number, and explained how he and Frank knew each other. It sounded pretty strange to me. We were convinced that this man had something to do with the murder. He knew so much about the crime scene.

We grilled him and investigated him, but he had an air-tight alibi, and we couldn't find any physical connection. The man couldn't explain his dream, only that he'd had similar experiences before involving friends in trouble. During our investigation, we spoke to his mother who told us he'd once dreamt that a friend's home was on fire in Montana. When he woke up in the middle of the night, he called his friend to learn that the bottom story of the man's home was, in fact, burning and that the phone call allowed the friend enough time to escape the fire.

We were later also able to corroborate his story with Frank's dad, who said on the morning before his son's murder, he received this man's phone call, grabbed a prayer card next to the phone, scribbled the message on it, and left it on the counter for Frank.

We were never able to track down another suspect or figure out what really happened to Frank. I still don't know how this man knew the things he did or where his dreams came from, but I think the case prepared me for events that would happen later in my life.

It was the first time I really considered the possibility of the supernatural. It wasn't until years later that I would learn about the spiritual realm and the war constantly raging around us.

MOTHER'S CARDBOARD COFFIN; CHILDREN FORCED TO CLEAN UP THE FATHER'S CRIME SCENE

During my time working homicide, death seemed to be coming at me from all sides. Not only was I facing T.T.'s mortality, every murder, drug overdose, and unfortunate or untimely passing in our city came across my desk. The Major Crimes detail I worked in dealt with the most heinous things imaginable. By that point, I'd responded to numerous homicides and witnessed some of the most horrific crimes scenes imaginable, but few affected me like the Smith family murder.

I got the assignment to investigate a strange call of suspected domestic abuse in a usually quiet and family-oriented neighborhood. In fact, it was the neighborhood where I now live. The suspect, John Smith, called in and said he believed someone had broken into his home the night before and hurt his wife. The man did not make much sense during his phone call to law enforcement, so we were already suspicious as we drove towards his address. I showed up to the home, along with another police sergeant, and knocked on the door.

"Police," we called.

No one answered.

We knocked again and identified ourselves, and again, no answer. We kicked in the door and began searching the house. My partner and I walked through the house room by room.

"It's clear!" He called out to me each time he entered a new door.

I responded similarly until we had covered nearly the entire house. I doubled back to a bedroom where I noticed a cardboard box in the middle of the floor. The box hadn't registered as anything unusual to me at first, but I decided to take a closer look. I walked towards it slowly and pulled back one of the panels.

I called to my partner, "I found her."

The young woman's mutilated body had been stuffed inside the makeshift coffin. She had been brutally beaten and slashed repeatedly with a knife until she was unrecognizable, but we knew it was Denise Smith. She was the mother of two boys, ages 9 and 11.

The details we uncovered through our investigation set her death apart from most others and would haunt me for years. Her husband had apparently believed she'd been having an affair, and in a drug-induced rage decided he was going to kill her. While the family was sitting down to dinner, John matter-of-factly told the boys his plan. He then proceeded to beat their mother with a baseball bat.

In the midst of the murder, he took a knife and slashed Denise's face and her body in several areas from her feet to the top of her head. After shoving her lifeless body into the box, John instructed the boys to go in and clean up the blood that had splattered onto the walls. I remember seeing the swirls of their small handprints in the smeared blood on the walls and being sick to my stomach.

The morning after he killed his wife, John sent his sons to school as if nothing had happened and called the police to report the crime.

John was convicted and sentenced to 27 years to life in prison. At the time, I felt that no punishment would undo the horror of what he did—not only to his wife, but to his two young sons, and I thought about them often.

Years later, I moved into that neighborhood, and it took me a couple years to be able to drive by that house. I always took an alternate route around it. I still do most of the time.

It is hard not to let cases like that get to you. The more time passed and the more gruesome the crimes I witnessed, the less I wanted to talk about it. I found myself internalizing a lot of the trauma I'd experienced. It may have been an attempt at self-preservation, but bottling it up only allowed the darkness to eat me up from the inside.

During that period and shortly after I divorced my first wife, I felt like death had taken a huge toll on me. I believed all the murders and death I'd seen had cost me my family and had taken so much of my soul. I felt compelled to display the pain on the outside.

I got a tattoo of the grim reaper next to a tombstone with the numbers "1-8-7," which is police code for murder.

Of course, my colleagues gave me a hard time for it. Some of the detectives in the Special Investigations unit (which investigated forgeries and other fraud cases) joked that they would get checkbook tattoos on their arms to portray the impact fraud had had in their lives.

We were able to find humor in the grisliest circumstances, but the reality was, many of my colleagues suffered from some form of post-traumatic stress injury. It would become part of my life's mission to help law enforcement officers and veterans struggling with the darkness they'd encountered on the job. But I couldn't save anyone from a life of despair until I was saved myself.

In the meantime, I was still trying to cope with my youngest son's illness while wading through the grotesque nature of my job working in homicide.

RICKY AND TINY

I continued to cover some of the city's most morbid cases, including the murder of Jackie, the owner of a second-hand dress shop. Jackie's body had been discovered inside of her shop, and she'd been stabbed repeatedly.

About two weeks after the crime, we got a tip that lead us to a local crack addict named Ricky. We believed he'd committed the crime but that he didn't act alone. We believed he worked with a woman who went by the name of Tiny. Despite her name, Tiny was a rather large woman, and she was no stranger to law enforcement. We were familiar with Tiny for her drug use and lifestyle.

During our investigation, we found evidence that the pair had robbed Jackie for about $60.00 before stabbing her numerous times. As we tracked the two suspected killers down, we were about 12 hours behind them everywhere we went. We knew they had relatives in Mexico, and that's where the investigation eventually led us.

We were able to locate Ricky and sent a couple of detectives across the border to talk to him. Unfortunately, because he or his parents were Mexican nationals, we were not able to have him extradited back to the U.S. However, Tiny was not from Mexico, so we worked with the Mexican police to have her deported back to the U.S.

Ricky initially claimed he didn't commit the crime but agreed to come back to the U.S. to talk to us. We had a warrant for his arrest, and as soon as he stepped onto U.S. soil, we cuffed him.

When we interviewed him later, he confessed to the crime. He was sentenced to life in prison. His attorney later claimed that we had forced him into the trunk of a car at gunpoint and brought him back across the border illegally. He threatened to have us investigated for kidnapping.

The case sparked several letters back and forth between the Mexican and American consulates, but it didn't take much to prove his theory wrong. There are cameras everywhere at the border.

Tiny, on the other hand, was only sentenced to three years on an accessory charge. I believed she received some mercy in this case, but for some people, despite the numerous chances they are given, they can't seem to break free of Satan's lies over their lives and they go back to the chaos of the world.

Several years later, she got into a fight with a boyfriend. Somehow she had ended up on the hood of his car. That didn't stop him from taking off. He ended up driving so fast that she flew off the car and was killed. Narcotics were found at the scene of this incident as well.

Day after day, I faced cases like Jackie's or of young children being molested or girls being raped or people meeting horrible dooms. I would find myself driving home with no emotion, no sadness, no hunger, nothing. I'd just be drained of everything.

I spent a lot of time trying to numb myself, and I started to cope with things by drinking. It became easier to process the monstrosities of many of the cases I was working on and the impact of my job over a beer with my colleagues, rather than to go home and deal with real life. But that meant spending more time away from home, which only exacerbated the strained family relationships. I can't help but blame myself a bit for Matt's addiction.

There is no excuse for my actions, but I can see how it happened. I'd look at so many others who'd gone through a divorce or had a broken family and think, "Why shouldn't I be divorced?"

The evil of the world's "normal" became acceptable in important areas of my life. Like his brother, T.T. struggled with addiction, but in his case, it was with pain pills. He'd been on and off hard-core pain medications since he was 12 years old.

He'd have to take the pills to cope with the cancer, but it often led to addiction. It seemed like every time he'd have an operation, he'd have to follow it with rehab. My own past struggle with alcohol brought me to a place that forced me to admit the patterns and frequency in which I drank impacted my sons.

I hadn't been setting a very good example. I was using alcohol to deal with my trials, and what message was I sending to my kids? That was my rock-bottom, and I stopped drinking altogether. Once sober, I realized there were several other areas in my life that needed to change. God continued to soften my heart, and I began to open up to the possibility of a real relationship with Him.

As usual, His timing was perfect.

CHAPTER SEVEN
SURRENDER

2 CORINTHIANS 5:17

Therefore, if anyone is in Christ, the new creation has come: The old has gone, the new is here!

SYLVIA CONFESSES TO MURDER ON A TALK SHOW

I know just how important timing can be; minutes can make or break a case. That became especially apparent during my assignment on the hostage negotiations team.

It wasn't like the movies, and we weren't always successful in being able to talk the bad guys down. Many times, the suspects involved in the call-outs were under the influence of alcohol or other drugs, and it could be very unlikely they were going to think rationally or listen to us.

This was the case in one incident that happened to be broadcast on national radio. The case began with a woman named Sylvia who was convinced she had multiple sclerosis. She would show up at the local MS Society office looking for help. However, workers there determined Sylvia did not, in fact, have MS, so they explained to her that they could not offer her their services. Sylvia did not take the news well and continued to show up and harass the employees at the office regularly. We had been called to deal with the situation before, but Sylvia took her grievance to the next level one afternoon when she showed up to the building with a gun. She shot at one of the employees as the victim was walking in the parking lot to her car.

Luckily, Sylvia missed. The victim called 9-1-1, but Sylvia was already gone when the police arrived on the scene. We began searching for Sylvia, but we were unable to find her right away.

Later that evening, I received a phone call from a nationally syndicated radio show. The person on the line asked me if we were searching for a woman who shot at somebody at the MS office. I said, "Yes." They told me they had Sylvia on the line and asked if we'd like to speak to her.

I asked, "Do me a favor, and please don't put us on the radio." They connected us, but of course, they aired the entire conversation.

I began by talking to Sylvia about her frustration with the MS Society and explained to her that she hadn't actually hurt anyone and the best thing she could do was turn herself in.

Sylvia had apparently been drinking and threatened suicide throughout the conversation. I was able to secure a confession during our talk, but ultimately, she hung up...before we were able to trace the call (the incident happened before cell phones, and the technology wasn't quite where it is today).

The next day, I received another call from the police department within a neighboring county about a homicide they were investigating. They believed Sylvia had shot a woman sometime the day before. They believed the victim was an acquaintance of Sylvia's, and for whatever reason, the two were at odds.

Investigators said Sylvia showed up to the victim's home while she was sitting on the couch watching TV and shot her through the living room window. I realized the crime must have happened between the incident at the MS Society and our phone conversation on live radio. Sylvia knew the whole time we spoke that she had killed someone and that she'd be facing serious consequences if she'd turned herself in.

I told the neighboring police about my very public failed attempt to convince Sylvia to turn herself in, but I thought she might make a repeat appearance on the radio that evening, and I warned the detectives to be ready. Sure enough, Sylvia called into the show. I was waiting, along with detectives from the other department, with hopes of tracing the call. Once again, the entire conversation went out over the radio waves. This time, the detective from the other department spoke to Sylvia. He got her to confess to the murder, and he also urged her to turn herself in. All the while, we tried to trace the call. Unfortunately, we were only able to determine she was in the L.A. area, but couldn't get an exact location.

On the third day, the LAPD got involved after Sylvia pulled a gun in public in their city. She was in her car when they pulled her over. Sylvia did not cooperate with police, and she ended up in a stand-off situation with the LAPD. For the third night in a row, the case ended up on the air. The radio station gave listeners a play-by-play as police attempted to talk

Sylvia out of her car and into their custody.

The story did not have a happy ending. Instead, Sylvia followed through with her threats of suicide. She shot herself in the head, and her demise was broadcast live to listeners across the country. Sylvia's was just one more case that took its toll on me.

I FINALLY SAW THE TRUTH: ONLY JESUS COULD SAVE ME

I was at my lowest point when I met my wife, Nicole (again, God's timing). I was coming out of my second divorce. T.T. was still battling cancer, Matt was still struggling with addiction, and I was still trying to keep up the illusion that I could handle it all.

Nicole invited me to a Christian worship band concert. I didn't care that it was a "religious event," I just knew I wanted to go out with this beautiful girl. Little did I know, the night of our first date would set into motion events that would change my life forever.

During the concert, a pastor spoke to the crowd, and his words hit me. I felt like he was speaking directly to me, and something inside me cracked. I finally saw the truth: Jesus is the only One who could save me. I decided then to seek the peace that the pastor spoke of.

There was one person I knew I could trust to talk me through it—my cousin Dan. He was able to explain Christianity to me in a way I could truly understand and walked me through the steps to salvation—accepting Christ died on the cross for my sin, asking Him for forgiveness, and committing to follow Him.

When I gave my life to Jesus, my circumstances

didn't change. My sons weren't miraculously healed. I continued to face challenges at work and at home, but I began to see things differently. I realized I didn't have to carry the weight of the world on my own shoulders. Jesus said to lay my burdens down at the foot of the cross, and that's what I did.

That is the beauty of God's mercy. He doesn't require us to "clean up" our act before we come to Him. He sent His son, Jesus, to die for us while we were still sinners. He found me and pulled me up out of that dark place. For God to be merciful and to use a guy like me—a broken guy headed for self-destruction in every area of my life—speaks to His character. He saved me from myself and my despair and brought me comfort that I had been desperately seeking in all the wrong ways.

It didn't happen overnight, but eventually, my relationship with Him brought me peace amid my suffering and, ultimately, a purpose in this life. Once I experienced His love, I found it impossible to keep it to myself. I needed to share it with my family, my friends, my colleagues, and anyone who would listen. I began to ask God to speak to me and to show me how I could serve Him each day.

Ministry doesn't simply happen in a church, and I learned I didn't have to have a title of "Minister" to have an impact. The Lord put me where He wanted me to be; I just had to be willing to listen.

God began to put me in situations that allowed me to witness about His impact on my life. In each case, the person I was witnessing to had opened the door to speak about faith and about the strength and peace He gave me during personal trials. Usually their trials were similar to mine. I was careful not to push my faith on anyone, but when the door opened, it would usually lead to prayer with people.

REPRIMANDED FOR SHARING FAITH ON THE JOB

One such case involved a woman who'd just hit and seriously injured a pedestrian with her car. The pedestrian had stepped out in front of her and changed her life in a split second. I offered her the comfort I knew only God could bring, and she accepted. A photograph of me kneeling next to her in prayer ended up on the front page of the newspaper. After the picture came out, one of my superiors reprimanded me for sharing my faith on the job. I was shaken, and I started to question whether I had overstepped my bounds. I knew that God presented me with these opportunities, but that conversation with my supervisor put some doubt into my mind. The very next day, I was working my shift as a motorcycle sergeant. I knew I was the last thing most drivers wanted to see when checking the rearview mirror. The flashing red and blue lights on my motorcycle signaled that an uncomfortable encounter with a cop was likely moments away. Watching me step off my bike and make the walk towards the driver-side window could be enough to ruin even the best day. But most people didn't expect to meet a cop like me. That was the case for Mary.

Mary was driving down a business area of town when she made an illegal U-turn. She obviously didn't see me behind her until I flipped on my siren to catch her attention. She pulled off to the side of the road and parked.

When I reached her window, I could tell Mary was more than a little distressed. After I asked for her ID and registration and discussed her violation, I inquired about how she was doing. With the threat of a traffic ticket looming, most drivers often answer, "Not good," or something along those lines. But Mary simply started to cry. As the tears ran down her face, she looked at me and said, "I'm just coming from the doctor's office. I found out I have cancer."

I knew I had a couple of options. I could add to her misery and write her a ticket, or I could open my heart to her by sharing my experience and ask Mary if she'd like me to pray with her. I went with the latter.

She looked up at me incredulously and asked, "Are you serious?!"

"Yes," I responded, "I am."

She agreed, and together, right there on the side of the road, we bowed our heads and prayed together. I don't remember exactly what I said. That happens a lot when I rely on God to produce the words, but I do remember Mary's whole demeanor changed after "Amen."

I reassured her that God was with her, whether she believed it or not. She thanked me and told me our encounter brought her much-needed and very unexpected comfort. I believe God used that incident to speak to her, but I think it was just as much for me. Having an opportunity to pray with someone while on patrol was a gift. God was reassuring me. He was telling me not to let the conversation of the day before discourage me. Of course, I didn't write Mary up.

If you had told me a decade ago that I'd end up sharing my faith with strangers on the side of the road,

I probably would have told you to get lost. But that was the old me. Today, I'm not afraid to share my story or my feelings. People who knew me before often have a hard time believing my transformation. But if my life teaches anything, it's that God can change even the hardest of hearts.

My journey has not been an easy one. It's been full of hardship and heartache, disappointment and despair, but it has also been full of grace and mercy, love and miracles.

After I became a Christian, Dan told me how close he'd come to giving up on me. He and his wife were concerned about the impact my choices were having on his own family. They'd been days away from giving me an ultimatum. They couldn't handle my past behavior and coping mechanisms and the drama it created.

My newfound relationship with Christ allowed me to deal with all the dirt I'd been holding onto. As for my kids, I learned that the only way to handle T.T.'s cancer or Matt's battle with addiction was to have faith and to rely on the Lord. I started backing off and stopped trying to be the problem-solver.

Instead, I just surrendered them to God. I tried to talk to my kids about my newfound faith, but they were the most difficult to reach because they knew all of my flaws. But they could also see the transformation happening in my life, and I believe that was more powerful than words.

As I learned to trust in God, my prayers for my kids began to change. Rather than praying for T.T.'s physical healing, I began to pray for his heart. He never confessed it to me when he was alive, but I believe God sent me messages to assure me of my son's salvation when I needed it most.

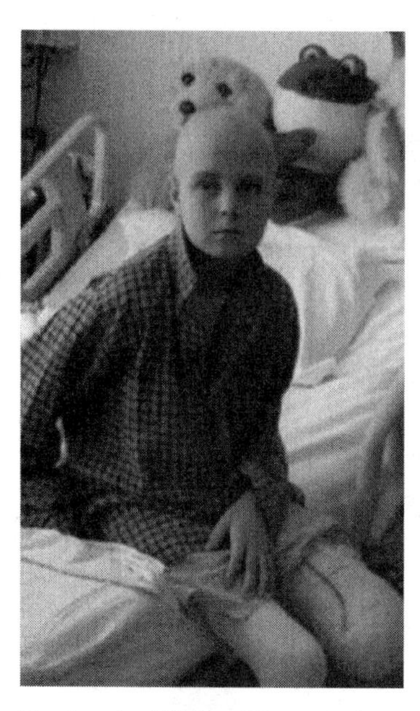

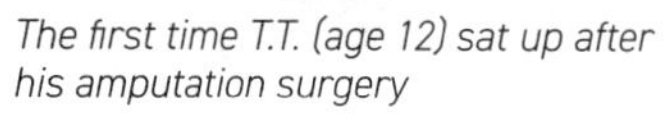

The first time T.T. (age 12) sat up after his amputation surgery

T.T. and my wife, Nicole, and dog, Rosie, at Cottage Hospital ICU

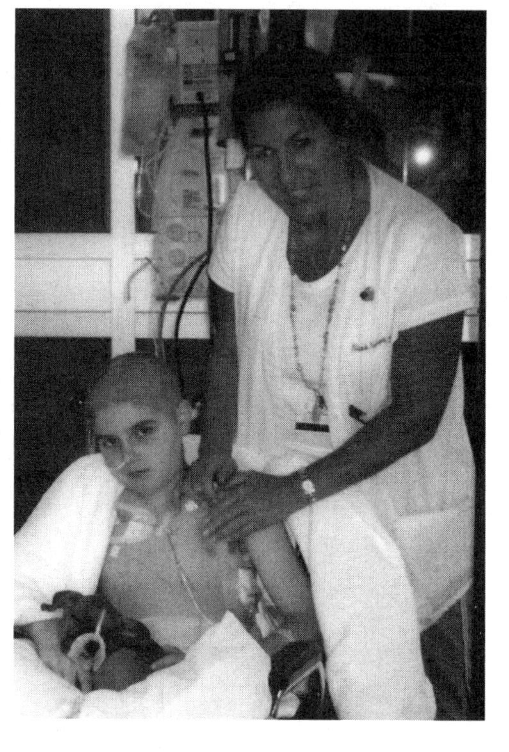

Me with my boys, Matt (middle) and T.T. (right) fishing in the Pacific

Me and T.T. when he was a toddler

Me with my dad, Fire Chief Warner McGrew

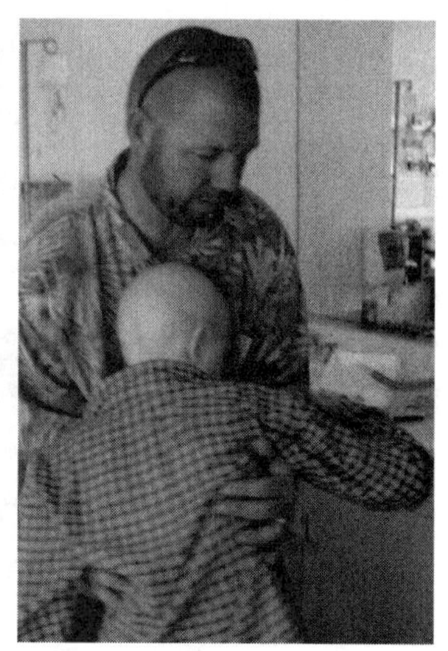

Me helping T.T. out of hospital bed following surgery

Me with T.T. on a bird hunting trip

Me with cousin Dan McGrew shortly after he joined the force

My daughter, Taryn, playing high school softball

My three children, daughter Taryn (left), and sons T.T.(center), and Matt (right)

Me and wife, Nicole, at social event

My swearing in ceremony with my dad (left) and then police chief (center)

Me teaching young T.T. how to shoot a BB gun

This photo of me praying with a woman following a car accident appeared on the front page of the local newspaper

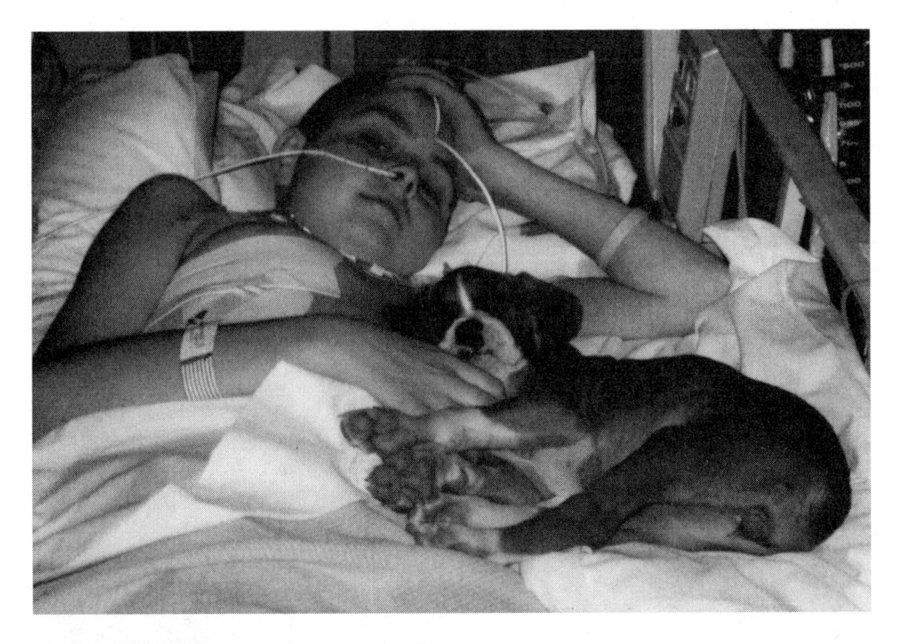

T.T. and Rosie the dog during ICU treatment

Me with my brother in Christ, Pastor Chuck Reed

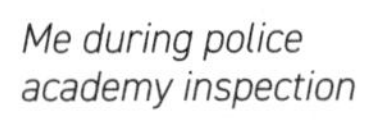

Me during police academy inspection

Me wrestling in high school

CHAPTER EIGHT

T.T.'S DEATH

MATTHEW 11:28-30

Come to me, all you who are weary and burdened, and I will give you rest. Take my yoke upon you and learn from me, for I am gentle and humble in heart, and you will find rest for your souls. For my yoke is easy and my burden is light.

T.T. MADE HIS FINAL GOODBYES, SAID HE LOVED ME; LATER, HE DIED

T.T. never got a chance to grow up or go on a date or just be a normal kid. How could he be normal? When other kids his age were worrying about getting acne or good grades, T.T. was in the fight for his life and watching as some of his closest friends were dying around him. That's what happens when you spend the majority of your time living in a cancer ward.

By the time he was 18 years old, he'd been through so much—the cancer, the amputations, and all the treatments. He'd endured 13 major operations and nearly died several times from complications stemming from the chemo.

Up to that point, his mom and I had been making the final decisions about his treatment, but I felt like it was no longer up to us. After his eighteenth birthday, I told him he could make all the decisions regarding his cancer treatments. I said, "You're a man now, and whatever happens, it's your call. If you don't want to go through another round of chemotherapy, I understand."

He apparently decided he was done with it all.

Months later, I was at work getting ready for my shift when I noticed several missed calls from my wife, Nicole, and a few other officers. They had left several cryptic messages for me to get back to them, but I had no idea what it was all about. Then a lieutenant called me and told me to report to the Watch Commander's Office.

I couldn't find the Watch Commander, but I ran into another officer who was in the room next to the office. I asked him, "Where's the Watch Commander? Why is everyone trying to get ahold of me?"

He responded, "He's over at a dead kid's house at 1234 Rose Garden Street."

My heart dropped. It was my ex-wife's address. Both T.T. and Matt lived with her at the time. As I rushed to the scene, I had no idea which of my two sons had died. When I got to the house, I walked through a sea of blue to get to the front door. Dozens of my colleagues (my second family) watched as I headed towards them.

I saw my ex-wife and went to her. "It's T.T.," she told me. She'd found him blue and lifeless, lying on his bed in his room next to empty bottles of his pain medication. He had written a note. A portion of the note read:

"I am truly sorry but I can't keep doing this.

I love you all. This isn't any of your fault.

It is my choice. There is just something in me. I can't explain it."

(Years after his death, I realized the significance of T.T.'s words. I would come to believe that T.T.'s battle involved something much more sinister than cancer.)

After reading the note, I felt the intense need to see my son. I walked towards his room. Even though I knew that it was my child on the other side of the door, I felt sorry for the other officers on the scene because I knew what they felt. I'd been in their shoes on numerous calls just like this one, and it never gets easier telling a parent that their child is dead.

The night before his death, I'd gone with T.T. to a meeting held at the local hospital for family members coping with alcoholism and addiction. He had called me and asked if I'd like to go, and I said yes. After the meeting, he said he wanted to go visit the nurses in the cancer ward. Many of them had become like family to him because he'd spent so much time with them throughout his battle with cancer. It didn't occur to me then that he was going to say a final goodbye. After that visit, he told me he loved me, and that was the last time I saw him alive.

CHUK'S PRAYER

T.T. had been sick for six years and had come close to death on a number of occasions, but I just wasn't prepared to lose him. At some point, one of the other officers asked me if I'd like to call a chaplain to the scene. I agreed and asked for Chuk Reed.

Chuk was home with his own son, who was also battling cancer and had taken a turn for the worse. Chuk selflessly decided to leave his ailing child's bedside to comfort me in my time of need. He was very aware that he, too, may be burying his son soon.

I believe God brought us into each other's lives at this exact moment for a greater purpose. Chuk helped me through one of my toughest moments, and I would soon have to reciprocate.

When Chuk showed up, he prayed with my family and me. I don't remember the words he said, only that they brought me immense comfort in the midst of the deepest despair I'd ever known.

On the day T.T. died, my cousin Dan happened to be receiving the same Award for Outstanding Performance or Valor that I'd received earlier in my career. Because of that, several of our extended family members were in town for the ceremony. That meant I had family to surround me on the worst day of my life (another example of God's goodness).

In the days after T.T. died, I leaned heavily on the Lord and on my closest friends and family. Despite being broken inside, I had to prepare to speak at my son's funeral. The service was open to the public, and about one thousand people showed up to say goodbye to my son. He had touched so many lives in his short time on earth. I believe God gave me the words to speak that day. It was the first time I would share my testimony with a large group of people. I also prayed God would help me remember the names of people who came to say goodbye to my son. I am typically not good with names, but I remembered each and every one that day.

ENCOUNTER WITH AN ANGEL

After T.T. died, I was broken, but I began to search for God's grace, and it wasn't hard to find. He sent me comfort in some of the most unlikely ways. The first involved Chuk. He had been in the room with my daughter Taryn and me before the coroner came to take my son's lifeless body away. I asked Chuk to pray for us, and he knelt on the floor and prayed.

Later when I went to thank him for his support, he asked about the woman with blonde curly hair dressed all in white who'd been sitting next to T.T. in the room with us during that prayer session. I assured him it had just been Taryn and me. Chuk was confident that she'd been there, and we praised God for showing him the vision of the angel of peace who'd been with T.T. in those moments.

A few days later, I received assurances from others who'd been present the day T.T. died. One of his therapists came to the house that day and asked to see him before they took his body away. She went into the room with him and shut the door. When she came out, she was pale and shaken. She said to me with conviction, "Mike, T.T. is with God!"

She repeated this as she trembled and held onto my arm. I smiled and said, "Thank you," and she left. It wasn't until a few days later that she told me what had happened in that room. She told me she'd been holding T.T.'s hand and saying goodbye to him when something took hold of her other hand and moved it in the sign of the cross across her body. The experience had visibly shaken her.

About the same time she shared her story with

me, Marty, a fellow cop and good buddy of mine, shared another unexplained occurrence he'd experienced on the day T.T. passed. He, too, was at the house that day.

"I'm not superstitious," he told me, "But, I gotta tell you what happened."

He said he'd been walking back and forth from the room T.T. was in and the driveway of the house and kept hearing a song he liked, but he couldn't figure out where it was coming from. He walked around looking for the source and then realized it was coming from his own pocket. He pulled out his phone and saw that the phone had switched to iPod, and then out of one thousand songs, it had randomly started to play "I Can See the Light," by Creedence Clearwater Revival.

The song happened to be by one of my favorite bands, and the lyrics held deep meaning to me. I knew it was God's way of letting me know T.T. had found the light and that he was with the Lord. I believe Jesus explained to my son in Heaven how much I really love him, and that brought me comfort. The Holy Spirit gave me those messages to encourage me through such a dark time.

My best friend, Matt, had a really tough time following T.T.'s death. He became depressed and his belief that God did not exist was strengthened because of yet another horrible tragedy in his life. He could not understand how God could allow his best friend to lose his child. Despite any of my attempts to change his mind, Matt could not recognize any hope in the situation. Before, I would have likely fallen into the same trap, listening to the enemy's lies, and for me, it would have resulted in turning to alcohol to numb the pain, but because I had God to lean on, I was able to experience the comfort only Jesus can offer.

People often blame God when bad things happen in their lives. They question His character or even His very existence when tragedy strikes. I have a different outlook. We are given free will. Without it, we could not truly love God. He doesn't force Himself on us, but He desires our love.

It is because of that free will that we are also able to choose the things of this world. That often allows the enemy to gain a foothold in our lives, and that opens us up to Satan's torment and attacks.

While God may allow it at times, I believe if we trust in Him, He will also use the attacks to strengthen us and ultimately pour out His blessings.

In Genesis 50:20, Joseph says, *"You intended to harm me, but God intended it for good to accomplish what is now being done, the saving of many lives."*

I love this verse because I see these words are true in my life. Because I opened my heart to the Lord, every attack that the enemy has launched against me, God has turned into a blessing for many people alive today.

Before I'd experienced His love, I'd likely get angry at God for putting me through trials. Now I have a peace that transcends all understanding, and I know He had a purpose for my pain.

CHAPTER NINE

FINDING PURPOSE IN THE PAIN

2 CORINTHIANS 1:3-5

Praise be to the God and Father of our Lord Jesus Christ, the Father of compassion and the God of all comfort, who comforts us in all our troubles, so that we can comfort those in any trouble with the comfort we ourselves receive from God. For just as we share abundantly in the sufferings of Christ, so also our comfort abounds through Christ.

YOU NEED TO TALK AND SHARE WHAT YOU ARE GOING THROUGH

Chuk said he watched me closely in the weeks after T.T. died because he knew he'd soon be in my shoes. His son lost his battle with cancer on a Thursday, just three months after T.T.'s death. A few days later, Dan and I decided to go to Chuk's house to offer him our support. We knocked on the door, and when it opened, Chuk stood there with a blank expression on his face. I reached for him, and he fell apart. He let out a loud wail and cried on my shoulder. He later told me it was the first time he had actually cried since his son had passed.

He had been taught that being the man of the family meant keeping emotions locked in tight, and he had been doing his best to emulate a pillar of strength for his wife and daughter. But I knew what he was going through. God had a plan for our lives and for each other in them. I knew how vital it was that Chuk give in to his grief.

"You need to talk and share what you are going through," I told him.

Somehow, knowing that we had that sorrow in common helped us both. I took Chuk with me to a hospice group I'd discovered after T.T. died. It was simply a room full of parents who'd also lost children, but it helped me to realize that I was not alone and that it was okay to let go and express my feelings and ultimately break through emotional barriers.

For me and for Chuk, the group allowed us to talk about our grief in a healthy way. Chuk describes it as being in a fraternity that we never would have signed up for, but one that has blessed our lives in such a powerful way.

Often in the middle of our despair or the midst of our mundane day-to-day existence, we are unable to see God's purpose for our lives. God taught us what it is to have joy in the midst of sorrow. Through my pain, God was so present and so gentle and so kind and so merciful. When people ask me, "What kind of God allows tragedy to happen?" I tell them, "God used my pain to forge me." It hurts to be forged, but the purpose is to get the impurities out.

I believe God used T.T.'s death to shine a light in the darkness of my life. In Chuk's words, "We couldn't have learned this type of grace in any course, conference, or seminar. There's no other way we would have got this understanding of life and death and what the Christian faith is about."

While the wounds of losing a child will never completely heal, both Chuk and I have been able to use our scars to help other families. Chuk began practicing grief counseling—something he says he never thought he'd be able to do.

As for me, T.T.'s death gave me more compassion for other families who'd experienced the same type of loss. I found the more open I was to Him, the more God put me in unexpected situations where I could share my testimony.

I AM NO LONGER JUST A COP DELIVERING BAD NEWS

In one case, it was supposed to be my day off, but while working an overtime shift, I got called to respond to a shooting suicide. When I arrived, I went into the young man's room. His body was splayed out on the bed, and he had a self-inflicted gunshot wound in his head.

Walking in on a scene like that is always disturbing and traumatic. As a police officer, most of us don't look at scenes like that and think, "Hmm, that's interesting." We look at it and see the heartbreak. We are disturbed by the senselessness of it. No person should have to witness such tragedy. For me, seeing the young man lying there also brought up memories of T.T. and the circumstances of his death.

I found this man's father pacing in the backyard, and I knew the life-changing grief he was experiencing.

He would never see his son again. I knew first-hand that there was nothing I could say to take his pain away, but I could point him towards the Lord, the only real source of comfort and mercy.

I began to talk to him about the circumstances of his son's death and shared with him that I, too, had lost a child to suicide. He asked me how I'd managed to survive the ordeal. That opened the door for me to share my story and how my relationship with Jesus allowed me to not only survive but to continue to find joy in this life.

The man admitted to me that he had once had faith but had walked away from it. After I shared my testimony, he asked me if I would pray with him. As usual, the Holy Spirit provided me with the prayer. I left the man there in the backyard. I knew my job was done.

Unlike before I'd become a Christian, I could now see hope in these dire situations. I knew God had equipped me to do the tough job because I'd done it so many times before. But now, I was also equipped with a testimony that I didn't have before.

Rather than dread going into a death notification assignment, I now felt honored that God might be able to use me to offer His love. Now, I could go into those situations knowing the Lord was working with the people involved because He was sending me (someone who'd been equipped with that same trial) to contact them. My heart still dropped when I got assigned to death notifications, but I also knew God was using me. I believe our testimonies have prophetic power. In this case, the Lord used mine to reach another man in the midst of what would likely be the darkest moment of his life and to offer him comfort, peace, and ultimately, hope. That is powerful. Maybe someday, this man would be able to do the same for someone else.

People may not want to hear advice, but they are almost always willing to listen to personal experiences. I don't have to preach or pressure them. I just simply ask if they'd like me to share my story. I've also found that people who are closed to sharing with me are more willing to open up to me about their experiences once they've heard mine. The floodgates open, and that usually leads to an opportunity for me to ask whether they'd like me to pray with them. More times than not, they agree, and God is able to step in to comfort them.

POINTING PEOPLE TOWARD JESUS CHRIST

Another time, God provided me with a powerful opportunity to share my faith during our annual Jeep trip. The retreats were a family tradition that had started when I was just a kid. T.T. loved loading up the truck and heading into the desert away from the "real world" along with a big group of other guys (mostly law enforcement officers). We would hit the 4-wheel drive trails during the day and sit around a campfire and tell stories at night. The year T.T. died, we canceled the trip. The following year, I decided to dedicate the trip to my son.

We had T.T. cremated, and I decided to scatter some of his ashes in the desert where we'd spent some of our best times together. We held a small ceremony to mark the occasion. I spoke about my son and what he meant to me and how the Lord had comforted me in my sorrow.

I shared with them John 14:1-4, which says:

"Do not let your hearts be troubled. You believe in God; believe also in me. My Father's house has many rooms; if that were not so, would I have told you that I am going there to prepare a place for you? And if I go and prepare a place for you, I will come back and take you to be with me that you also may be where I am. You know the way to the place where I am going."

This scripture gave me so much comfort and spoke to me in a way that promised me that T.T. was in Heaven because of the tremendous sacrifice of Jesus and that Jesus had lovingly accepted my son into Heaven.

Sharing my faith among that group was a bold move. Many of the guys that go on the trips are not only not Christians, but some actively deny God as I did before. But as my relationship with the Lord grew, I became more comfortable sharing it with others, and God continued to bless me as I stepped out in faith.

In the years that followed, and even today, the Jeep trips continue to present opportunities to talk about the Lord and share what He's done in my life with some of the people who are the most important to me. The men that have known me since I was just a kid have seen my transformation over the years, and that example is more powerful than any words.

I figure, in my line of work, we point people towards rape crisis or domestic violence services when they are needed. I think offering God's love is similar if someone asks for it. As I began opening myself up to the Lord, He faithfully put me in situations where He could use me. I began feeling the Holy Spirit's urging to pray in specific circumstances.

Sharing the story of T.T.'s death is still very painful for me, but I have also seen how it can impact other people. I have met with other parents who've lost children. They often ask me, "Will this pain ever go away? How will we survive this?'"

Because I've been through it, I can tell them what Jesus did for me. I don't tell people, "This is what you should do."

Instead, I am able to come to them and simply say, "This is what I did."

I can point to Jesus and say, "He is what got me through."

My story has been comforting to others. In that, I am able to see a purpose for my pain.

About two years ago, I was on patrol near a local retirement home. I noticed a rough looking guy with tattoos and a long beard. He looked like an outlaw biker, and my first hunch was to shake him down and see what he was up to. I started watching him and determined that he worked at the retirement home. God put it on my heart to go pray with him.

At first, I think I made him a little nervous when I walked up to him, but it turned out he was a really nice guy going through a hard time. We started a conversation, and he told me he'd been pretty bummed out that day. He said his kid had cancer, and I knew God had led me to this man. It was just one of those connections. There was this guy having a bad day and just trying to keep it together. I asked if I could pray with him, and the Holy Spirit led a prayer for comfort for him.

More recently, I received a call from an old family friend, John. John and I met on one of our annual

Jeep trips, and our boys had spent time together on these trips. Like T.T., John's son had a life-threatening illness, so we naturally bonded during the time we spent together. While I was in the middle of writing this book, John's son passed away at just 23 years old. John immediately reached out to me.

While he did not call himself a Christian, he allowed me to pray with him and his wife. I continued to pray for them in the weeks following their son's death, and the Lord quickly answered my prayers. John sent me this text message:

"I can't imagine the brutal treatment regimen you are going through (referring to my chemo treatments at the time). You inspire me to find the joy in life again. I know it can come, but it seems so distant. I've always been one of those guys that was always to the far left of what I call 'Jesus Light.'

Now I find I need to let Him in. Brad's passing doesn't make sense, but it seems the only explanation I will find is by letting the Lord into my life."

John went on to tell me he'd found a Bible study group that had helped him to open his heart to the Lord and thanked me for spreading God's love. Being able to use my pain to help someone else makes it easier to bear. God would continue to reveal to me just how powerful a person's testimony can be.

CHAPTER TEN

LETTING GO

PROVERBS 3:5-6

Trust in the Lord with all your heart
and lean not on your own understanding;
in all your ways submit to him,
and he will make your paths straight.

JESSE AND THE BOOMERANG PRAYER: HE WAS NOT THE MURDERING PAROLEE THAT I HAD LABELED HIM AS. JESSE WAS A HURTING CHILD OF GOD

While on patrol one day, I received a call about a suicidal subject. Arriving on the scene, I realized the subject was Jesse, a former gang member and convicted killer I'd arrested over 20 years before. Jesse got into a fight at a party and stabbed his victim. He turned himself in weeks later and served his time in prison. He had been out of prison for a while when he attempted to kill himself by slicing his wrists. The paramedics had already loaded him onto a gurney and were wheeling him toward the ambulance when I recognized him. He was creating a lot of drama with the paramedics as they rolled him past me, and I couldn't help but have a negative feeling toward him. "Hey! You ever think about quitting being a hoodlum?" I asked. He yelled back, "I'm not a gang member anymore!"

I prayed for Jesse as the paramedics were working on him. They had him in the ambulance when God told me to go to the hospital to pray with him. I didn't really want to and upon arriving at the hospital, I drove around the block three times before I gave in and went inside. I asked Jesse if he remembered me, he replied, "You're the cop who arrested me for homicide."

I told him how I ended up in his hospital room, asking if he would be willing to pray with me. He agreed, but as I prayed for him something unexpected happened. I realized that God did not have a message for Jesse. He had a message for me. God showed me that Jesse was no longer the murdering parolee that I had labeled him, but was a hurting child of God. I realized it was my heart and my perception that needed changing. I had judged Jesse the minute I realized who he was. I was wrong. I am only called to love him like one of God's children. That's the thing—it is important to realize that God accepts us for who we are and loves us all. We simply have to accept Him, and it is God that does the transformation. We don't have to do anything.

God instructs us to forgive. He sacrificed His only son so that we can be forgiven. In the Bible, in Matthew 18:22 (NLV), Jesus is asked how many times we should forgive others for their transgressions against us, He answers, *"I tell you, not seven times but seventy times seven!"*

We may think that a person deserves God's

wrath, but the truth is we do not know what is going on in the heavens. I believe we shake up the foundations when we choose to forgive. God is bigger than we can ever fathom, and His justice is so much bigger than we can understand. It is easiest to pray constantly and let God do the rest. I'll say it again, His willingness to meet people where they are, no matter what they've done in their past really speaks to His character.

I think people make it difficult when they try to change themselves. Despite our faults, we are all capable of becoming new creations in Christ. It is life-altering when we can look past our own impressions of or differences with others and begin to see them simply as fellow daughters or sons in Christ. I find that when I try to be better for Him, it doesn't work. It has to come from Him. It's an everyday effort and so important to find that connection each day. It can be a struggle. The enemy wants to keep us distracted and sidetracked, but the more we are in constant contact with God, the more He will work in our lives. People can be so hard on themselves about their past, but they need to know not to let that hold them back. They need to know that Jesus died for their sins and while people might bring up the past, God does not do that.

MY CHILDREN BELONG TO GOD, AND I AM NOT GOD

God continued to teach me compassion and understanding for others through my relationship with my son Matt. Dealing with Matt's battle against addiction gave me a new compassion and empathy for other families in similar circumstances. In the past, I tended to look down on them or judge them. Now I share my heart with these parents of children who have overdosed or are in jail for addiction-related crimes. Their world is unraveling, and I can say, "I know what you are going through." Sharing that my own son has been battling an addiction changes the dynamic. I am no longer just a cop in the room.

People often think we, as parents, cause our children's problems, and therefore we can or should fix those problems. I've learned the only thing a person can do is have faith in God to handle it. I know the rides parents go on with their kids. When Matt was sober, I felt good, but when he was using, it put me in a bad place. Matt's battle against addiction was similar to T.T.'s cancer battle in that it was life-threatening and horrible, but also something over which I had no control. The greatest lesson I had to learn was how to lovingly detach from Matt and love him without enabling him. It took years to learn that and requires constant reminding.

The first time we took Matt to rehab, I thought, 'This is it. He'll be fine. He'll do the time and be cured.' But that wasn't the case. In fact, it was just the beginning of the whole thing. He has been through many programs since then. Once out of rehab, he stayed sober for a while, but it often seemed he could not make it past 90 days.

I spent quite a few years trying to help Matt and support him in different areas, but was I really helping him or simply enabling him? It wasn't until I found a relationship with Jesus that I was able to let go. Through prayer, I realized that my son is God's child. As much as I love him, God loves him more than I ever will. Once I realized and trusted that, everything changed.

I have a great understanding of God's love, not because of something I did, but because I have experienced it. His love took away a lot of my pain and the burden I carried. I was immersed in Matt's situation, but God gave me patience, love, and understanding which resulted in more peace.

I vividly remember the day Matt was in a really bad place, and I was sure he was going to die. I thought, "I cannot bear to lose another son." I was driving along the coast as the sun was setting when I was reminded of the story in Genesis when God asked Abraham to sacrifice his only son, Isaac. As excruciating as it was, Abraham obeyed and went as far as placing Isaac on the altar before God stepped in and offered an alternative sacrifice. I pulled over, got out of the car and spoke to God out loud, "He's yours, God. Just take him. If this is the story of Abraham and Isaac, so be it. I've experienced this once already. I know the pain, but I trust you with my son!"

The moment I gave God my trust, He gave me strength to do what I needed for my only living son. A few days later, I was on patrol and happened to see Matt sitting on a curb. He was living on the street and didn't look well. When I pulled up next to him, he asked, "Dad, can you just feed me, or let me stay with you tonight?" In the past, I would have agreed. Instead, I did one of the hardest things for a parent to do. I said no. "Buddy, I can't. If I clothe you, house you, or do anything else for you, you're not going to do what you need to do to get out of this situation." He wasn't angry when he said, "Yeah, you're right."

As difficult as it was to do, I drove away feeling

a new sense of peace and trusted God with my son's situation. God put it on my heart that I'd done the right thing. A few days later, Matt got himself into a program. He made the move. In the past, it had always been me picking him up and saying, "Let's go do this." For the first time, it was all his doing.

The program he found required him to spend a year in Colorado where we had family, and he stayed with them when he completed it. For a while, things were going really well, but unfortunately, like all the times before, he lost track of his goals and did not stay sober.

No matter how difficult it was to watch my son relapse, I never for one second stopped loving him. Some days his actions caused me pain, and I felt like I could not take any more, but not loving him was just not an option. That is how God loves us. He is faithful to us, even when we are sinful or fail to spend time with Him. He never falters. My relationships with my children helped me to understand that in a real way. I know how deep my love is for my kids and that God's love for me surpasses that. I know this because He was willing to sacrifice His only son for me. The gravity of that is not lost on me because I know what it is to lose a child. I would not have gone through that willingly.

It is probably because of my understanding of God's love that I feel so strongly about following Him. As I write this book, Matt has returned his life to the Lord and has been restored in many areas of his life, including his sobriety. Matt continues to receive God's grace and blessings and is renewed in Jesus. My son has allowed me to share this portion of his amazing testimony which has been woven into mine.

He believes our transparent testimonies hold power that will help others. I believe this as well, and I am reminded of Revelations 12:11, which tells us of how the saints will overcome Satan: *"They triumphed over him by the blood of the Lamb and by the word of their testimony; they did not love their lives so much as to shrink from death."*

I ASKED GOD TO SOFTEN MY HEART

Late one night when working an overtime shift in the downtown bar district of our city, I monitored a serious radio call go out on the other side of town. I headed to the area and started searching for the parties involved. Dispatch advised they had been contacted and there was no longer a need for me. I was driving down a dark street away from the area when suddenly a man stepped in front of me and flagged me down for an unrelated incident. He directed me to a man and woman arguing near a moving van parked down the street. When the man saw me approaching, he ran around the van away from me. I exited my patrol car and ran after him. When I caught up with him, I saw that he was attempting to dump narcotic paraphernalia. I grabbed his arm, and he stiffened up, and for a second I thought that we were going to go to blows. I yelled for him to sit down. He hesitated but sizing up the situation decided to sit on the nearby curb. As I asked him for his information, he exclaimed, "I know who you are!" I replied, "Who am I?" "You're McGrew. Nicole's husband." At first I was a little taken aback, but when he said his name was Jeff, I recognized him. He had grown up with my wife. She told me his story and how nice he was to her, but his battle against drug addiction had led him to a life of crime. I knew then it was not a weird coincidence that we met that night. It was a divine appointment.

I asked God to soften my heart toward the man who I nearly went to blows with minutes before, and let the Holy Spirit guide me. Jeff told me he wanted to get clean and sober, was tired of living on the streets and then shared his faith with me. I arrested him for possession of the paraphernalia, and at the station, I explained to him that his offense was a misdemeanor. I then told him that I would issue him a citation and would work with him if he made the steps to get into a local rescue mission rehabilitation program. I witnessed to him about the Lord's love for him and asked if he wanted to pray. We prayed together, and God again provided me with the words that brought the hope of Jesus' love to Jeff. I released him with a conditional citation and invited him to attend church with my wife and me.

At home that night, I told my wife the story. "God really is working in you, isn't He?" she asked. Nicole knew all too well that the old Mike would never have shown compassion to this man in such a way. In the following weeks, Jeff attended church with us, and I could see the spiritual battle that was occurring. He could not sit still in the church. He walked in and out of the service, confronting the demons that tormented him. He attended a few more Sunday services but eventually went back to the streets where he was again arrested and sent back to prison. This was disheartening to both my wife and me, but we knew the only thing we could do for him was pray. Years passed before our paths crossed again. In those years, Jeff was not only imprisoned in the physical sense but was dealing with spiritual bonds. God is present in even the worst circumstances. The enemy may attack, but the Lord can turn it into blessings. The next time we met, I was better equipped to help Jeff in his battle.

CHAPTER ELEVEN

THE POWER OF PRAYER

JAMES 5:16

Therefore confess your sins to each other and pray for each other so that you may be healed. The prayer of a righteous person is powerful and effective.

KEVIN TURNED OUT TO BE AN ANSWER TO PRAYERS

I met a locksmith named Kevin one day while getting a key made. He was a large black man, about 6'4' with a muscular build. "How are you doing?" I asked. "Not good," he replied. After a bit of conversation, he told me his son had recently been murdered in a drive-by gang shooting in Los Angeles County. I told him I understood because I, too, had lost my son, adding, "The only thing that helped me through it was God." I started witnessing to him, when he cocked his head and said, "You know, I used to be a pastor." Our encounter spurred him to return to his life in ministry. The next time I saw him, Kevin would help to bring peace to a tumultuous situation.

Years went by after our meeting at the locksmith. In the summer of 2014, the fatal shooting of Michael

Brown in Ferguson, Missouri, sparked protests around the country, including our city. About 500 people gathered at the local courthouse to demonstrate. To keep the public safe while the people marched in the street, police blocked off the roads using what is termed a rolling barricade. We also tried to guide the demonstration route away from the freeway to avoid shutting down traffic or having any of the protestors or passing motorists seriously injured or killed. I was the motor sergeant and in charge of organizing the barricade. The plan was to keep the protesters moving along the downtown main street. It was obvious that many of the protesters did not like the police, and I prayed for the safety of the crowd, the cops, and the city. The Holy Spirit heard me and brought me peace as I led the officers who guided the crowd. Unfortunately, at one point, the crowd got around the police barrier and turned up a side street toward the freeway onramp. They moved closer and closer to the freeway, and we had to increase police presence. As a result, the crowd became more unruly and the threat of impending violence more evident.

The SWAT team was on standby in a nearby parking lot and assigned to block the roads with the armored vehicle and police cars. Officers were prepared in riot gear including batons, shields, and less lethal munitions. The crowd continued to advance toward the police barricade, and some protestors became physical by pushing on the police shields. Things were heating up fast. We were preparing for a riot.

This is when I saw a figure walking back and forth between the cops and the protesters. His intimidating stature caused the people to back off. He was creating a space between us. Then I recognized him. It was Kevin! He was separating the crowd from the police and literally standing in the gap. When he got close enough to me, I reached out and grabbed his arm. "Do you remember me?" He stopped, "Yeah I remember you." I said, "We have to turn this crowd around." There was an understanding that passed between us at that moment, and he added, "This is about Jesus now." Somehow he convinced the crowd to head in the other direction toward the police station where they held a peaceful talk with police leadership. Kevin was just one of many answered prayers, and that divine encounter has led us to be good friends to this day. Kevin later told me that the reason he was in that crowd was because God told him to go there and walk with the protestors for the safety of the community. I am thankful for my friend's obedience that night.

As I matured in my faith, I began to get more aggressive in my prayer life and to listen more closely to the Lord. He began presenting me with situations that took me way out of my comfort zone and began breaking down my own ideas of what it meant to be a follower of Jesus.

ANGELS IN ATTENDANCE? AN OFF-DUTY NURSE, PARAMEDIC, AND SURGEON SHOW UP AT THE ACCIDENT

Charlie, a retired police sergeant and long-time friend, and I were driving back from an annual quail hunting trip at a ranch he owns in Arizona when we witnessed a dramatic crash. A young woman driving in front of us at about 80 miles an hour swerved in an attempt to miss a tire in the road. She lost control of her car and hit the center divider before rolling several times. I did not think she had survived. We pulled over, jumped out of the car and ran across the freeway to help her. Miraculously, she was alive and was sitting behind the wheel, looking dazed, her seatbelt still strapped in place. Her only apparent injury was a small cut above her eye. I told her to stay put while we called for an ambulance. Waiting for the paramedics to arrive, I began to pray. A few minutes into my prayer a nurse showed up. She examined the girl, and I continued to pray. Soon a man pulled up, an off-duty paramedic who happened to have all of his gear with him. He and the nurse checked the girl out, but I didn't stop praying. Moments later, a man identifying himself as a flight surgeon arrived on the scene. Within minutes of the crash, he and the other two were able to assist the girl, all before the paramedics arrived. Fortunately, the young woman was just a little banged up and ultimately okay.

I approached the girl before we left the scene. "I need to tell you that was a horrific crash. It's a miracle you survived. I was praying for you, and God didn't just send help. He sent a nurse, a paramedic, and a surgeon. If you're doubting whether God is with you, I want you to know He is." Her jaw dropped, and I could see the emotion on her face as she acknowledged the supernatural way the events unfolded.

God's presence in my life continued to become increasingly clear. I learned to look for the spiritual in the day-to-day. The more open I was, the more God revealed. I didn't always get it right.

A few years ago, I was driving home from Colorado after visiting family and made a stop in Arizona to pick up a few things from a store. I pulled into the large parking lot and noticed it was empty. I purchased what I needed from the store and walking back toward my truck, a man approached to ask if I could give him a few bucks to pay for a couple of quarter pounders with cheese. My initial response was, "No. I'm sorry, I can't help you."

I walked to the driver's side of my truck, but something stopped me in my tracks. God put it on my heart that I needed to help the man. The inner struggle only lasted a few seconds, but when I turned around to reach out, the man was gone. It wouldn't be so strange except, as I mentioned, the lot was empty. There was nowhere he could go. It was as if he had just vanished into thin air.

I immediately felt conflicted and couldn't get the man off my mind the entire drive home. I felt I had blown an opportunity to entertain an angel and I prayed to God, "I'm sorry. I feel like I just blew it." I remember the experience whenever I feel God urging me to step out of my comfort zone. A year later, God gave me another opportunity to reach out to an angel.

PRAYING WITH AN ANGEL; THIS TIME, I DIDN'T HESITATE

I went to a local coffee shop to get my wife a peppermint mocha. As I walked into the coffee shop, I was met by a man walking out who grabbed my attention. The man with bright blue eyes smiled at me, and I smiled back. He was in pajamas, and I thought perhaps he was a patient at a surgery center across the street from the coffee shop. I picked up my order and was walking toward my truck when I noticed the man standing in the driveway of the parking lot and immediately felt God urging me to go to him and pray. Remembering the man in the Arizona parking lot the year before, this time I didn't hesitate. I approached and asked how he was doing. He said he was okay, but had been dealing with a long-term medical condition and some other difficult circumstances. "I can relate," I assured him.

I told him about T.T.'s long battle with cancer and the emotional hardships that came with his long-term pain management. What I didn't tell him was that my son Matt had been diagnosed with a life-threatening heart condition that kept his heart working at only 25 percent of its function. We were told the condition was caused by an earlier illness that had done irreversible damage to his heart. He would never fully recover and all that could be done was to manage the symptoms. I continued to talk to the man and eventually, I asked if I could pray for him. He agreed and resting my hand on his shoulder, I prayed for his healing. The strange thing is when T.T. was sick a lot of people offered healing prayers for him, but I saw no evidence that it worked. I believe in the healing powers of Jesus and in the power of prayer, but at that time I just never thought healing prayers were for my family or me. I certainly never expected to be the one praying for healing for someone else, but then like so many times since dedicating my life to Jesus, I found myself doing something I never imagined.

Following the prayer, the man thanked me and I

walked back toward my truck, but something prompted me to immediately turn back to say goodbye. The man was gone. Just like the day in the Arizona parking lot, there was nowhere the man could have disappeared to that quickly.

A few hours later, I was out running errands when Matt called me. "Dad, I need to tell you something. I went to the cardiologist earlier today and he said I'm healed." The doctors couldn't explain it. It was a miracle. It was then I was convinced the man I'd prayed with earlier that day was an angel. I relayed the incident in the parking lot to Matt, concluding, "I was obedient, and it was God that healed you."

God's miracles are so personal and unique to each one of us that when they happen, we can be certain of what they are. They have God's signature all over them.

CHAPTER TWELVE

THE GIFT OF PROPHECY

1 JOHN 4:1

Dear friends, do not believe every spirit, but test the spirits to see whether they are from God, because many false prophets have gone out into the world.

GOD BEGAN REVEALING HIS GIFT OF PROPHECY TO ME. MY PRAYER BECAME, "LORD, SEND ME, NO MATTER THE COST."

When we open ourselves up to the Lord and ask Him to use us, He does. When my spiritual journey began, I was unopened to God. Then I acknowledged Him in my desire to find peace and blessings for myself. Once I received those things, I started to have more faith. Soon, the Holy Spirit moved in me, and a shift happened. It wasn't about me anymore. Instead, I desired to be a servant.

My prayer became, "Lord, send me, no matter the cost." I became accustomed to talking with God through prayer, but it was still a big surprise to me the first time He audibly spoke back. I was driving back from a trip to L.A. after attending a police department leadership school when I heard God's voice. He said, "Mike get off the freeway. Go to the Christian bookstore. I want you to buy a book."

His voice was clear. When He said my name, it was so loving, like He knew every piece of me. It was powerful, and I knew it was God. But, I just kept driving. As I passed the next off-ramp, He said again, "Mike, get off the freeway. Go to the bookstore and buy the book." I doubted myself, thinking, "This is crazy!" The third time He spoke, it was in a stern voice. He said, "Mike, GET. OFF. THE. FREEWAY. GO. TO. THE. BOOKSTORE." I listened. I had to backtrack a few exits to get to the bookstore, which could not be seen from the freeway, and once inside I prayed, "God, I'm here. Now what?"

He led me to three books. The first was about prophecy and the role of modern-day prophets, and the second two dealt with spiritual battles. I began reading through the books. It became apparent to me that God was preparing me for the next phase of my journey.

First, He began revealing His gift of prophecy to me. I began to really listen for His voice, and He began showing me things through dreams and visions. The purpose of prophecy is to edify and exhort the church and to comfort man (I Corinthians 14:3). The testimony of Jesus gives us the authority to speak into the lives of others who are suffering similar trials that we have suffered and to help bring them God's grace. I also believe that prophecy allows us to speak God's will into the heavens so that His will is done in Heaven and on earth.

I noticed that God done this with my testimony on many occasions. Each time I testified about His influence in my life and the supernatural miracles He showed me, I was releasing a prophetic word that caused people to focus on God, increase their faith, and receive the comfort that comes from God through prayer, fellowship, and the presence of the Holy Spirit. Whenever I am placed into a situation that deals with a person going through an extremely sensitive or heartbreaking situation, I pray for the gift of prophecy, and God has never failed to give me the appropriate words to help the person focus on God and receive His comfort.

I also began to learn to listen to the different ways that He speaks to me, which includes his language of unusual circumstances that can either be received as being from Him or dismissed as some worldly coincidence. I have learned that each time I recognize a divine encounter with another person, God wants me to step in and be open to giving the person a word that comes from Him.

One day I was in the San Francisco airport on a layover when a woman sat down next to me who had a striking resemblance to Sara, the co-author of this book. Sara was pregnant and within weeks of her due date at the time, so I decided to pray for blessings for her and her unborn daughter. In the midst of my prayers, God told me He also had a blessing for the woman in the airport. "Go," He said. Unsure about reaching out to this stranger, I obeyed. I walked up to the woman and told her about God's blessing, "He is with you," I assured her. The woman's eyes lit up. "Thank you so much! I really needed that. You don't know how much!" she responded. I walked away, but later when boarding my plane, there she was again.

She was the attendant on the plane! She approached me during the flight. "What prompted you to give me that message?" she asked. "God just sometimes tells me to do or say certain things, and I was just passing along what He told me," I replied. She explained she was experiencing several trials in her life and needed those exact words at that exact time. I watched as she focused on God and began to ponder what had happened. It was obvious that God touched her, but he also touched me in a big way. God gave me another message for her during the flight, and when I departed from the plane, I passed the message along. "You are very special to God, and He is going to use you in a powerful way," I explained. That was the last I saw of her, but I praised God all night for once again showing His glory to me.

These incidences happen to me fairly often. God gives me the words to speak that comfort people or bring them peace. According to Jeremiah 33:3, God uses this gift to reveal "great and unsearchable" things to come, and I Corinthians 14 tells us that we should all pray for the gift of prophecy. This gift builds and strengthens the church. Most people don't have these experiences often, although God wants us all to prophesy and pray for this gift.

I believe God has selected me for a purpose, and I am willing to answer His call and serve Him. We are all equal at the cross. I believe God has called me to release words into the heavens and into people's lives. He uses my testimony of Jesus. When people hear my story, my prayer is they walk away focused on the Lord, not on me.

FALSE PROPHETS LOOK FOR WAYS TO TAKE US AWAY FROM GOD

On the contrary, Satan uses false prophets and similar tactics to steer people away from God. He is very complex in his attacks, but it's very simple—he wants to take the glory and us away from God. He doesn't have the power to kill, but he'd love nothing better than to wipe us all out. He can, however, convince people to harm themselves or others. He is the father of all lies.

He doesn't come out and say, "Hey, it's me, Satan. Follow me." He does things that mimic God but mock Him at the same time. He often disguises himself, tweaks God's Word just enough for it to be damaging, and cons people into believing his lies. He can use demons that have been around forever and know all about us, our ancestors, and our family lines, and they know the curses that have been put on us. They follow our families down the lines, and they look for ways to take us away from God. Often their most effective weapon is using false doctrines or making evil trite.

Satan also uses other abominations to God, including mystics, mediums, and psychics.

Often, they know they are working for the enemy. They seek spiritual gifts, and they get them. They commune with demons, and they get a sense of power from that. These people are attractive to others who are seeking some spiritual connection, inner happiness, comfort, or purpose in their lives.

In one case, a famous TV personality known for her psychic abilities came to our town for a conference. I was assigned to work security at the event, but I felt very hesitant to do so. A fellow officer, who also happened to be a Christian, urged me to go anyway. He told me that God wanted to use me and show me something at the event. He was right. When I got to the theater where she would be performing, I met with the other security guards assigned to the event. Two of them were also Christians, and we prayed together to bind the enemy from doing his work.

As people began to show up, I noticed a young girl with a bald head, and I was immediately reminded of T.T. and the young kids he spent time with in the cancer ward when he was growing up. I knew how vulnerable she must be, and I imagined she and her family were there to try to make sense of her situation. She was an easy target.

This young girl was facing death, and she was seeking some sort of comfort or guidance from this celebrity. The enemy would offer the dying girl some commercialized alternative to what happens after death. It was very disheartening.

The young girl wasn't alone. There were about two thousand people, the majority of them women, who showed up in hopes of having their fortunes told or to gain some communication from "the other side."

As the program started, I began to pray. Then a very interesting thing happened. The prayers to bind the enemy had an impact on the celebrity psychic. Each time she would leave the stage to target an audience member, she would take a path as far from me as possible. If I would move around the room, it was as if there was a polar effect or a bubble she could not penetrate.

Each time she would attempt to read someone's

fortune, I would pray to bind the spirit, and often, she was unable to get through. She had picked up on me and continued to keep her distance throughout the program.

I believe these false prophets are, in fact, communing with the spiritual realm, but rather than speaking to the deceased loved one, they are receiving information from demons.

After the performance ended, several men approached me and explained to me that they were only there because their girlfriend or wife had dragged them. It showed me that the enemy is really attacking women, and it made me realize just how much we need a strong women's ministry in our area. I would also later come to realize how powerful women can be in ministry.

I believe the experience with the celebrity psychic taught me a lot about how the enemy works and how powerful the name of Jesus can be in the fight against evil.

We have the Bible to guide us, but we also have Jesus. People may find some worldly comfort in other things, including alcohol or drugs or other "spiritual" experiences, but that comfort is only temporal.

One day, my wife, Nicole, was out shopping when a woman confronted her. The woman referenced Nicole's aura and seemed to know personal things about my wife. She also noticed that Nicole carried her stress in a certain area of her body. The stranger urged Nicole to focus on her "self- care" and offered to help her do so.

My wife wasn't interested, but it brought something to my attention. Often, these alternative spiritual experiences do focus on one's self.

That is contrary to what Jesus teaches. Instead, He commands us to pick up our cross and follow him. That isn't what most people want to hear. Most are more interested in the "what's in it for me?"

But again, I believe these alternative experiences open up the doors for demons to come in.

I still had a lot to learn, but God would soon bring people into my life who would teach me more about spiritual warfare.

THE LURES OF THE ENEMY; SPIRIT GUIDES OFFER PROMOTION TO NEXT LEVEL IN DEMONIC ACTIVITY

In the midst of writing this book, Ken, brother of Frank, the unsolved murder victim mentioned earlier, came to me and shared his story. "After my brother's death, I became very angry at God," he told me. "As time went on, and his murder remained unsolved, I began searching for my own answers." Ken experimented with "energy" focused belief systems, and religions not God-inspired. He eventually tried tarot card readings and saw power in them. He hung out with a New Age group who introduced a "spirit guide" into his life. A spirit guide is a demon usually unexpectedly received by people through trickery. Ken's spirit guide was called Drake, which he later learned is the Anglo version of Dracon, meaning Dragon (prophetic meaning Satan). Ken was introduced to a warlock who told him about a book of demons he possessed. The man said he used the book to seek revenge on people who had done him wrong and offered to let Ken utilize the book for vengeance on anyone who harmed him. Ken recognized, at this point, that he was being invited to the next level in demonic activity and decided to reject the offer and turn instead toward the power of the Lord. Ken has since become a powerful member of the prayer team within my current ministry (which I will discuss later in this book) because of his transformation in Christ and past knowledge of the devil's schemes and wiles in the new-age movement. Just as God began to reveal Himself to me in very real ways, He eventually allowed me to come face to face with the enemy.

CHAPTER THIRTEEN

ENCOUNTERS WITH EVIL

II CORINTHIANS 4:4

The god of this age has blinded the minds of unbelievers, so that they cannot see the light of the gospel that displays the glory of Christ, who is the image of God.

SPIRITUAL WARFARE: MY FIRST EXPERIENCE WITH DEMONIC ACTIVITY; LIKE A SCENE OUT OF *THE EXORCIST*

For most of my career, I saw the struggle between good and evil as it played out on earth, but I've since learned our biggest enemies cannot be seen by human eyes. They are in the spiritual realm. I believe if we could unveil our eyes, we might possibly see angels and demons fighting it out over people's souls. Cops meet people and see things in humans that simply cannot come from the normal human brain—evil that could only be Satan-inspired. After I acknowledged the supernatural fight, it became very real to me when God introduced me to my first battle with a manifested demon.

A number of our officers were called to the scene

of a man with a gun. A fellow sergeant, Todd, and I were left with just a handful of personnel to handle the rest of the city. We received a call that a homeless man was passed out in front of a local business, and the business owners were concerned about his well-being. It is unusual for two sergeants to go out on patrol together, but we were the only officers left to handle the situation. We found the man in bad shape, lying on a grassy patch of ground. I said, "Hey buddy, we're getting some complaints, and we need you to get up and move on." When I got a closer look, I could see the back of his pants were covered with blood. He had been bleeding internally and had an ashen glow about him. I asked him whether he was feeling okay. He said, "No, my stomach feels pretty messed up." We immediately called an ambulance.

We talked to the man while waiting for the paramedics to arrive. I was considering all the medical issues he could be suffering. It did not occur to me that his affliction might be caused by spiritual forces. Eventually our conversation shifted to faith. I asked the man about his relationship with the Lord, and he said he once knew God, but walked away and had been living on the streets for some time. I asked if he wanted me to pray for him, and he said he did.

I was preparing to pray when I smelled the odor of death. I know, as I have been around countless deaths throughout my career, that there is no mistaking that smell. At the same time, my police radio began blaring traffic and my phone started to ring. As the distractions increased, I turned to Todd asking, "Do you see what is going on here?" He nodded yes. It seemed pretty clear to us that the enemy did not want me to pray for this man, but placing my hand on the transient's shoulder, I prayed anyway. As I did, a demon manifested. It contorted the man's body in unnatural ways. It was like a scene out of *The Exorcist*. I had never experienced anything like it before, and I didn't know how to cast out a demon. I never expected to need to know, but I had read the books God told me to buy at the bookstore and so I had an idea where to begin. I started to pray and the Holy Spirit stepped in and gave me the words to say. I prayed in Jesus' name, and as the demon went out of the man, it raised the upper portion of his body in contortions off the ground. Once it left the man, he fell back to the ground. The man's entire countenance changed. The color returned to his face, and he looked as though a huge weight had been lifted from his shoulders. He looked like a different man. He started to fervently pray himself.

The ambulance arrived, and one of the paramedics sniffed the air. "What died?" he asked. I said to the paramedic, "It's a long story." I later went to the hospital to check on the man, but he had already been released. I don't know what happened to him, but I believe the Lord used this experience to open my eyes to the reality of the spiritual realm in a way most people have to see to believe.

After we cast the demon out of the man, Todd and I acknowledged what had happened and prayed for protection for ourselves and our families. It was an intense situation. Later that night I went to a place of worship to pray about what happened, and during that worship time, I had an amazing experience. I felt the Holy Spirit fill my soul. I didn't hear my own voice when singing. It was like the Holy Spirit was audible through my vocal chords as I was praising God. I believe I was experiencing baptism in the Spirit, as discussed in the book of Acts.

My head was spinning when I left the worship service. This was different from the physical water baptism I had received before. God had walked beside me when I wasn't a believer and saved me from all the perils and dangers I faced on the streets. I once believed I was the one who got myself out of those situations because I was a good cop. But it wasn't me. It was God the entire time. Then the Holy Spirit was allowed to dwell in me when I received Jesus Christ as my Lord and savior. That night God poured His Spirit out on me, and it changed everything for me and continues to do so. In the days that followed, I felt the strong presence of the Holy Spirit, and I believe that because I had the Holy Spirit with me and because I had become a threat to the enemy, I also became a target. I began to have spiritual encounters that I never would have expected before that first experience with the transient.

I was off duty and in plain clothes, walking along a downtown street when a woman I had never seen before came walking on the sidewalk toward me. She was carrying a number of shopping bags, but when she saw me, she set her bags down on the ground and started to walk into the busy, traffic-filled street away from me. It was as if there were an unseen barrier between her and me. She walked around me in the street as I passed, staying focused on me as she snarled and said things that were personal about me, but she would not come near me. Not sure what was happening, I called out to her to get out of the street before she got hit by a car. I suddenly realized that the woman was demonized and said a prayer to bind the spirit then continued on my way.

A male transient singled me out on the street the following day and yelled, "Get that spirit out of here! Get that spirit out of here!" Again recognizing what was happening, I prayed to bind the enemy, and the man left. It is a powerful thing if you're walking in the Holy Spirit. The enemy sees that, and the spiritual realm will make its presence known.

It is important to recognize the enemy is present in the world, but it is more important to recognize that God has given us all the tools to fight Satan and the authority in the name of Jesus to defeat him and his works. The Bible talks about arming ourselves against the evil forces of this world. Some Christians ignore this, but I believe we should take these passages to heart. The more willing and open I was to fighting spiritual battles, the more often I was confronted by the enemy, and I wasn't alone.

SEEING THE ENEMY: AS A COP, RUN-INS WITH EVIL ARE COMMON

Sergeant Todd shared a story with me about a case he'd covered that left him shaken. He responded to the scene of a suicide in which a young man had overdosed inside his car. When Todd arrived, he looked over the scene to be sure there were no suspicious circumstances. He noticed the color of the young man's hair—light brown—and the color of his clothing. As he was taking in all the details, he glanced back at the body and instead, saw his son.

He jumped back and blinked hard. When he looked again, it was the young man he'd seen initially. But the experience broke him. He walked back to his car, got into the driver's side, and cried. He felt the anguish and grief as if he had, in fact, lost his son.

He heard God's voice tell him, "Pray for this man's family." He knew that they would soon be notified of their loved one's death, and they would need comfort. As he prayed, he felt a sense of relief wash over him. When Todd described the story to me, we agreed that we are fighting a battle most people are not willing to acknowledge.

I have been involved in several officer involved shootings as either the investigator, supervisor, or by being present when the shooting occurred. In one case I was present while handcuffing the downed suspect who had attacked an officer with a deadly weapon.

The man was dead, but per policy, we have to place handcuffs on the suspect, even if they've been injured, or in this case, shot. As we rolled the man over, he had the most evil look on his face. I'd never seen anything like it before.

The officer who'd shot him still had his gun drawn. He was visibly shaken. I walked over to him and helped him to holster his gun and walked him to the car as other officers awaited the paramedics.

I asked the officer, who happened to be a fellow believer, if he'd like me to pray for him, and he agreed. God gave me a prayer for protection against the evil one, and I could sense the battle wasn't over.

After I brought the officer back to the station, the enemy continued to come after my colleague. The suspect was also a possible gang member, and the officer began to be overwhelmed with fear that the fellow gang members of the man he had just killed might come after him or his family. I have found that the enemy wants to create and magnify fear to levels that will break a person. Satan continued to torment the officer. We prayed again for protection, and he received peace.

At times, it is nearly impossible to walk away from some cases without seeing the darkness going on. There are times it seems the criminals are reaching out for help. If you turn your back, they might kill you, but their spirit is crying out because the devil has them in his grasp.

One case that stands out involves a 15-year-old boy named Manuel. I was working as a Patrol Sergeant when we were called to break up a gang fight in a residential neighborhood. Most of the kids involved had scattered by the time we arrived, but I caught one of them. When I grabbed him and asked, "What are you doing?" he started to cry. This is the reaction you expect from a 15-year-old, after all, he is just a kid. I sat him down for an impromptu heart-to-heart. He admitted he only did the things he did because of pressure from his friends. I advised him, "There are only three ways out of the gang life: jail, death, or you get yourself out." He agreed and promised to straighten up, so I let him go home.

A week later, we responded to another gang fight downtown. There were about 100 people involved, and it was chaos. We were short staffed that day, so I told the officers to just start grabbing whoever they could. We got a report of a kid down in the midst of this insanity and found the boy in a bush in a department store planter. He'd been stabbed to death, and when I saw his face, my stomach dropped. It was Manuel.

We tracked down the kids who had stabbed him, and they, too, were only teenagers and showed no remorse. It is in these moments I see the enemy hard at work. Satan is alive and very active in our world. He is on a mission to steal, kill, and destroy as much as he can before his inevitable end, but we have authority over him in the name of Jesus Christ, the one who died on the cross for our sins. Somehow, most people find the latter difficult to accept.

WE ARE CALLED TO FIGHT: STORM THE GATES OF HELL

These experiences spurred me on to further study spiritual warfare. Scripture tells us that Jesus wants us to use His authority to cast out demons in Matthew 10, and He goes on to tell us that the gates of hell will not prevail against His church in Matthew 16:18. The Word tells us in Ephesians 6:10-12 *"Finally, be strong in the Lord and in his mighty power. Put on the full armor of God, so that you can take your stand against the devil's schemes. For our struggle is not against flesh and blood, but against the rulers, against the authorities, against the powers of this dark world and against the spiritual forces of evil in the heavenly realms."* I believe God wants us to put on His armor because we are called to fight and not just sit back and get pummeled by the enemy. He wants us to storm the gates of hell and destroy the devil's schemes.

The more I learned about the spiritual realm, the more I reflected on T.T.'s suicide note. In it, he lamented, "There is just something in me. I can't explain it." I now believe he had been tormented by the spirit of death. I did not have the tools to recognize it at the time or to help. God would soon bring people into my life to teach me how to help others dealing with the same spiritual struggles as T.T. had. Again, I believe God used my pain to prepare me for the plan He had for me.

CHAPTER FOURTEEN
RAISING AN ARMY

EPHESIANS 6:13

Therefore put on the full armor of God, so that when the day of evil comes, you may be able to stand your ground, and after you have done everything, to stand.

PEACE AND FREEDOM FOR TROUBLED COPS

My work as a police officer brought me to my breaking point. As God began to heal me, He allowed me to recognize that many of my colleagues were suffering as I had. Whether it be with substance abuse or other vices, it was happening too often within my own department. I realized that in so many cases, Satan had a hold of many of my fellow officers. That is when God revealed to me a new purpose for my own life: to save as many others as possible.

Cops take the things they see home, and it has a negative effect if they don't have a healthy outlet. In fact, several studies show that cops are more likely to commit suicide than to be killed in the line of duty. I have personally seen it happen on more than one occasion. In addition to the physical and emotional nature of the job, most officers work atypical hours with graveyard shifts and only have days off during the middle of the week when most civilians are working. This means a cop can go weeks or months without spending any quality time with friends outside the force.

Six months on the graveyard shift can make anyone crazy. On top of the sleep deprivation, the overnight shift often includes late-night pursuits, bar fights, and other disturbing calls that get the adrenaline flowing not usually encountered on the day shift. It can be tough to put the previous night's work out of mind and get some sleep when a cop goes home. If sleep does come easily, it's not a good sign either because it means the things that should affect you simply don't anymore. All that to say, the job takes its toll on the men and women who vow to protect and serve.

Like war veterans, many law enforcement officers suffer from some form of post-traumatic stress injury. Unfortunately, if an officer seeks medical treatment through the department, it goes on their record and can impede future promotions within the force or ultimately cost them their job. Consequently, many officers find alternative ways to deal with the trauma—usually alcohol or other unhealthy habits.

Because of my journey, my story, and when I started openly sharing my faith, people often came to me to talk about the issues they faced. I realized we needed to do something to change police culture. God put His call on my heart, and I could not ignore it. One night I had a vivid dream involving cops and first responders. The men and women in uniform were rising from the dead. God later put the scripture Ezekiel 37 on my heart, which describes God breathing life into dry bones and raising up an army. I knew He was calling me to minister to my brothers and sisters in blue, but at the time, I didn't know exactly what I could do to make a difference. Naturally, He didn't leave me in the dark long.

IRON SHARPENS IRON

God brought Michael Hammer into my life at just the right time (as usual). Michael is the only grandson of world-renowned industrialist and philanthropist, Dr. Armand Hammer. Michael not only inherited the responsibility of the Hammer legacy but has been extremely successful in his own business ventures and gives away much of what he earns.

I was serving as the president of the local Police Officers Association, and I had been working on a plan to help my fellow officers cope with post-traumatic stress. I tried to stand up for the needs of the department, but I knew I could do more. I began by putting together a program to help address the emotional needs of local law enforcement officers outside of the typical channels. Beyond that, I knew I wanted to take a faith-based approach because I knew how powerful it could be.

Of course, creating such a program was going to cost money. We began fundraising and received a generous donation from Michael's family's philanthropic foundation. Later, I happened to see a video of him speak at an event and was blown away by his faith and the way he chose to use his money to further God's kingdom. I felt compelled to reach out to him and let him know that his money was being used to honor the Lord.

Michael agreed to meet with me, and it wasn't long before we realized we had a lot in common. We'd both lived a worldly life before finding the Lord. Michael, too, had experienced God's grace and the spiritual realm in a very real way. We shared our stories of faith and quickly became close friends.

Michael also expressed his lifelong respect and appreciation for the men and women who served our country, whether in the military or in law enforcement. He told me he wanted to do whatever he could to help get my plan off the ground and running. He told me to begin gathering the people and resources I would need and that he would help to support the program.

About that time, a friend and fellow sergeant, John, came to me with a serious emotional issue.

He said, "Mike, I'm so heavy I can't even breathe."

(John was the officer who'd shot and killed the young man strung out on meth several years prior. He was now working as a sergeant in the homicide unit.)

Although years had passed, he said he was still grappling with effects of that day.

He told me that each case he worked brought him back to the tragic events of that day. The impacts were not just mental and emotional, but physical, too. His anxieties were keeping him from being able to qualify with firearms. Each time he fired his weapon in the range, the sound of the gun shot and the smell of the gunpowder brought him back to the day of the deadly incident.

As police officers, we are required to pass testing, including shooting at a firing range, every few months in order to remain on duty. He was worried that he would no longer be able to pass and could lose his job. I could see that the enemy was again creating needless fears in John's head and magnifying them to the point of extreme anxiety.

I decided to introduce John to Michael in hopes that John could benefit from talking with Michael about the counseling project we were working on. Michael has a special gift to be able to give people a Holy Spirit-inspired testimony of God's love in order to bring peace and wisdom to them in times of need. He allows the Holy Spirit to speak through him and by doing so, has brought me God's peace and revelation many times. It is always a powerful experience when we fellowship together, and I felt John needed to experience the same fellowship with Michael.

When they met, Michael was able to have a tremendous impact on John. Michael strongly recommended John go see a Christian counselor in Orange County who had helped him during a particularly difficult time in his own life.

The counselor's tactics were a bit unorthodox, but Michael assured us that he could get to the root of the problem in a way most therapists could not. That is because this counselor focused on spiritual healing.

The counselor's name was Pastor Jim Hanley, and he would not only provide help for John, he also taught me a whole new way to approach spiritual warfare. Sergeant John would eventually receive freedom and peace through Pastor Hanley's program.

The introduction also spurred the ministry that

would later become my calling. Through prayer, God began to form a team around me who would help to launch the life-saving program.

SATAN CAN'T DEFEND AGAINST THE POWER OF LOVE; PRAYER METHODS IN SPIRITUAL HEALING

It didn't take long to see how desperate officers were for such a program. In addition to Sergeant John, men and women began coming to us seeking help. We helped dozens of people within the first year. It was all about saving lives and keeping cops healthy, but it was also an opportunity to steer people towards the Lord.

Even if someone wasn't seeking spiritual healing, they could receive secular counseling, but there were always Christian counselors available. The idea was to have God's hand on the program at all times.

We also began a separate prayer ministry. That's where Jim became instrumental. He taught me and other counselors prayer methods in spiritual healing—a much kinder way to deal with demonic oppression.

When I first saw the enemy manifest in the transient, the fight to rid him of the demon was violent. Jim taught me a new approach to spiritual battle, including the power of love.

Love is one of the greatest weapons we have in the fight against evil. Going through and dealing with the wounded parts of a person and bringing healing to them is a loving act. Love disarms the enemy. Satan can't defend against love.

Spiritual healing involves praying with the afflicted person and disabling any footholds and strongholds Satan may have in their lives in a very loving and gentle way. It is very different from my first experience casting out a demon.

The goal is not to freak people out or traumatize them. Instead, when I pray with people now, the demons don't fight much because they know they don't have any power. We deal a lot with people who have post-traumatic stress injuries. People can experience inner healing when they deal with stuff they've been hanging on to. We also often see people who've inadvertently invited the enemy into their lives by dabbling in New Age or other spiritual systems.

The ministry is effective because it deals with the issues themselves and gets to the wounded parts, and once you expose those things and let the Holy Spirit guide the process, it weakens the enemy. Satan loses his rights and his grip on the person. At the end of a session, when you cast out a demon, there is no big fight. They know they've already been defeated. Then the person can experience freedom. It's the power of love, and it's a loving approach all done in the name of Jesus.

It may be hard to understand, and many people do come into the first prayer session with at least some skepticism, but that usually dissolves quickly when they experience freedom.

In the case of David, a combat war veteran, demons continued to show him the people he'd killed in combat. He had tried numerous counseling sessions, but nothing seemed to free him. He was being severely tormented, and the torment was destroying his life. He learned about our program through a mutual friend and asked if he could set up a session as a last resort. It only took a few minutes to call out the demons who'd been tormenting him—"death" and "rage," to name a couple. Within an hour of strategically directed prayer, we cast the demons out in the name of Jesus Christ.

I continued to work in the deliverance ministry when God brought a believer in need to my front door. My wife's friend Jeff, whom we'd taken to church several years before, had served his sentence for drug use.

Several months after his release, I began to hear on the streets that Jeff was not doing well and that the drugs were overcoming him once again. In the midst of working on this book, I was in my house taking a nap after going through more invasive cancer-monitoring tests. I heard a loud knock on the front door of my house. I opened the door, and there stood Jeff.

I was surprised to see him standing at my front door and had no idea how he knew where I lived, but I could see that he was hurting, so I invited him in. Jeff told me about an experience that had shaken him up and about his last run on the streets and the torment it brought him. He asked me how he could have a spiritual awakening and draw closer to God.

He wanted deliverance from Satan's hold on his life. I explained inner healing and deliverance and then prayed with Jeff. Jeff broke free of the enemy through the inner healing prayer and casting out the demons that had been tormenting him. After the deliverance, his countenance completely changed. Since that time, Jeff has grown in the Lord and is seeking Him in a powerful way. We continue to fellowship and pray together, and it's wonderful to see the transformation and miracles that God is doing in his life.

I find that often God's plans take time to be revealed. Something that seems awful at the time may result in unimaginable blessings.

Spiritual healing is an ongoing event. At the end of the day, you still have to go to that still, quiet place and let the Lord minister to you. On my son's most recent release from a rehab program, I felt the need to say a prayer choosing to forgive him. I didn't realize I was hanging on to so much anger or resentment but saying that prayer let the floodgates open. God cleanses us when we confess our sins and unforgiveness. That's usually the biggest thing the enemy uses against us—unforgiveness—because it's so easy to hold onto without realizing it. We can even hold it towards our loved ones.

What I've learned about forgiveness, whether dealing with criminals or someone who's wronged me, is that it applies to everyone. The book of 1 Samuel tells the story of David and Saul. In it, David was presented with an opportunity to kill Saul, a king who had threatened his own life. Instead, David showed Saul mercy and said to him, "May the Lord judge between you and me. And may the Lord avenge the wrongs you have done to me, but my hand will not touch you."

I believe if somebody wrongs us, we can stand in the way of God's justice if we don't have forgiveness in our heart.

Ultimately, I believe this ministry is God's fulfillment of the prophecy He sent me about the valley of the dry bones. I believe there is healing happening in our department and among the other men and women who seek treatment through the program.

CHAPTER FIFTEEN

JOY!

JAMES 1:2-4

Consider it pure joy, my brothers and sisters, whenever you face trials of many kinds, because you know that the testing of your faith produces perseverance. Let perseverance finish its work so that you may be mature and complete, not lacking anything.

RUN OVER BY A METH-CRAZED RV DRIVER

In July of 2015, a few months before I was diagnosed with colon cancer, I was working patrol and monitored a call for a domestic dispute in a motorhome. The victim had been beaten up by her boyfriend, Brett. She escaped, but Brett took off in the RV. Officers located him and pulled him over, but when they ordered Brett out of the vehicle, he refused to comply. I was listening to the whole thing go down on my patrol radio. "The subject has locked himself in the cab of the motorhome," the dispatcher stated. I could tell things were not going well and decided to go to the scene to help out. By the time I arrived, things had escalated. Brett had blood streaming down his neck and onto his chest. He had apparently tried to slit his own throat with a knife. The wound wasn't life-threatening, but we called paramedics and continued our attempts to coax him out of the vehicle. It was clear he wasn't coming out, and we needed to go in after him. He still had the keys in the ignition, so we decided to put police cars in the front and the back of the RV to block him in. I approached the driver's side window and had my younger cousin, officer Dusty McGrew, use a glass pick to shatter the window. I then thrust my baton against the shattered glass to remove the broken pieces so I could reach in and unlock the door. I quickly pulled the door open. A fellow officer tased the crazed and bloody suspect. I managed to grab ahold of Brett, but he fought back. He somehow managed to start the engine and threw the RV into reverse. I heard the gut-wrenching crunch as he slammed into the cop car parked behind him. He then put the RV in drive and, once again, the sound of metal on metal as he rammed into the patrol car parked in front of him. I was struggling to pull him out of the RV when he turned the steering wheel toward me, causing one of the vehicle's wheels to run over my right foot. I lost my grip on him, and he continued to alternate gears until he maneuvered around the patrol cars. The other officer who'd tased Brett still had a grip on the driver-side door. "Let go of the RV!" I shouted to him. I could see that Brett had no intention of stopping, and I didn't want my colleague to get dragged along.

The wheels made a screeching noise as the RV peeled out into traffic. Brett was going about 60 miles an hour down a very populated residential area. The last thing we wanted was a meth-crazed, suicidal subject driving through traffic and endangering the public, so we didn't push a high-speed chase scenario. It was a big motorhome, and we could see it even a few blocks away, so we simply followed from a safe distance. I prayed no one would get hurt as Brett proceeded through the city. I could feel the adrenaline coursing through my veins as I watched him sideswipe a school bus carrying about 25 kids. By this time, there was a motorcade of cop cars following the runaway RV, several in pursuit and the rest responding to the havoc Brett was wreaking on the city. In addition to the bus, Brett ran into several cars and caused a motorcycle officer to crash his bike. Miraculously, no one was seriously hurt. We continued to follow the RV with an officer responding to each crash he had caused. We would have been justified in using lethal force to take out the suspect in this case, but by the grace of God, it didn't come to that.

Eventually, the RV engine died, and Brett was forced to stop with me close behind. I jumped out of my car and ran to the motorhome. Several other officers joined me, and we surrounded the suspect. Brett must have realized he was cornered and had no other way out because he finally stepped out of the motorhome with his hands in the air. We approached Brett, placed cuffs on his wrists and placed him under arrest.

Once Brett was safely in custody, I drove to the hospital to check on the motor cop who had crashed during the chase. His family was there and were obviously shaken by the incident. I prayed with them for comfort before heading back to the station. That is when the adrenaline began to wear off, and I felt the impact of where the RV had run over my foot. I was wearing boots and was not looking forward to taking them off to see the damage. Sure enough, my foot was broken in three different places. The injury put me out of commission for three months.

For the second time in my career, I was awarded the medal of valor for the RV incident (the same award I received at the beginning of my career for taking down the samurai sword swinger). However, this time I wasn't looking forward to the ceremony. I had avoided the annual event since Dan received the honor the day T.T. died. I was filled with anxiety when I learned I was to be honored. The ceremony brings back a lot of emotions for me stemming from my son's death. I had to rely on my faith, God's grace, and His love to get me through it. After the ceremony, a man approached me to tell me his friend's daughter was a friend of T.T.'s and had actually had a bit of a crush on him. The man said her father told him that she had recently been having vivid dreams of T.T. in heaven. In her dreams, T.T. was alive, healthy, and happy. The message hit me hard. I knew it was a message from God, once again reassuring me T.T. was in Heaven.

NERVOUS BUT OBEDIENT; PUBLICLY SHARING MY STORY

About this same time, I had committed to speak at our city's annual prayer breakfast. Although I was hesitant to share my story of faith to a room of hundreds of people, I knew God wanted me to do it, and I'd been working on obedience. My speech was God-inspired and God-infused, and when I had the chance to watch a recording of it later, I knew I couldn't have given the same speech on my own.

Again and again in the Bible, God uses the weakest or least likely people to carry out His plans. The book of Judges describes Gideon—considered among the weakest of his family—who was chosen to save his people.

Once again, Israel had rejected God, and He allowed them to "suffer for their sins." They were driven out of the Promised Land by the Midianites. Rather than supply a huge army, God had Gideon take a small group of just a few hundred men to defeat the vast Midianite army.

What set Gideon apart? The Bible describes him as "a man of faith." He trusted that the Lord would do as He promised and provide His people with victory, despite how unlikely that was.

The more I trust in God, the more He is able to use me. I may not hear God speak to me every day, but I believe He is using my life, like so many before me, to show people, "Look! You don't have to be perfect to be a part of My plan!"

My foot eventually healed from the RV incident, and I returned to full duty. About a month later, I went in for a routine colonoscopy. That is when I received the cancer diagnosis.

The chemo really kicked my butt. I think the enemy was trying to use the cancer and the resulting chemotherapy to take me out. The three-day-long treatments started out with a blood draw so doctors could determine if my body could handle another round of intravenous poisoning. When doctors gave the okay, I'd get plugged in through a catheter in my chest. Then I'd just have to sit and wait for the side effects to kick in. I imagined I would feel the same way after sucking on the exhaust pipe of a running car for an hour.

The nausea was often debilitating. My skin and teeth became insanely sensitive to cold, and I developed sores in my mouth and on my skin. The doctors prescribed medication to help with the nausea. Prayer—my own and others' on my behalf—also helped me deal with the other side effects of chemo. Doctors told me the reason the chemo affected me more than most was likely due to my size (I am 6'3" and over 250 pounds) and the higher dosage I required. But the doctors also reassured me that the worse the chemo made me feel, the more likely that it was doing its job, destroying any residual cancer cells floating around in my body.

Going through my own journey with cancer often brought me back to my son's fight with the disease. It was hard not to think of him on the days when the chemo was really kicking my butt. I realize that it must have been even harder on his young body. I find myself reflecting on the time we spent together in the pediatric cancer ward.

I knew that my suffering was temporal and that God was going to use my trials for some good, although it was tough at times to see what that could be.

Even as I went through the cancer and as the chemo was trying to break my body down, God was strengthening my inner man. That's what He does. The Holy Spirit walks with us. He convicts us at the right times. He's so faithful.

I completed my chemotherapy, and in the midst of writing this book, I was declared cancer-free. That seemed like a pretty good way to wrap things up, but

God had even bigger plans in mind.

PROMOTION: NOT MY WILL BUT THINE BE DONE

While I still had some healing to do (a person has to recover from the chemo because it can be almost as damaging as the cancer itself), I knew I'd be heading back to work, and I put in for a promotion from sergeant to lieutenant. It seemed like the logical next step in my career.

I went through the grueling application process, which included an interview with our department's new chief (whom I hold in high esteem). The interview seemed to go really well, and I figured with all my experience on the force, I had a pretty decent shot at the job.

I prayed that God's will would be done and received peace. God also placed the Bible verse Psalm 37:4 on my heart, which says, *"Take delight in the LORD, and he will give you the desires of your heart."*

At first, I thought it was God's assurance that I would get the job I'd applied for, but God knows my heart better than I do. Instead, it wasn't me who got the promotion. My cousin Dan got the job. I was extremely proud and happy for Dan, but I was left wondering what God had been trying to tell me.

As I pondered what God was speaking to me, He then made it very clear and told me, "YOUR HEART'S DESIRES."

It hit me like a ton of bricks. I had never prayed for the lieutenant position; I had prayed for God's will. My earnest prayers were for blessings for my loved ones and that the programs I had dedicated to

God's kingdom would be blessed. I prayed that God would use the programs to bind the broken-hearted and to free the captives so that His army would be strengthened and that His will is done on this earth as it is in Heaven. I prayed that my heart be filled with His desires and that I'd be one with Jesus. I was filled with excitement! God was about to show me His Grace again!

Shortly after Dan's promotion, the Chief opened a new sergeant position that had not existed before. This position would be in charge of different specialty details to include the chaplain program that had previously been reduced to one chaplain. I competed for the position and was selected.

I began to rebuild the chaplain program and have been able to intertwine it with the other program that God had previously put on my heart. I was then assigned to work solely on a wellness program for the entire department.

God had placed me in a position so that I could receive, as the song says, "Thy fount of every blessing, tune my heart to sing Thy grace!"

After 30 years in the same profession, I was excited about taking on a new job that would require me to learn new things and face new challenges. I would also be able to do the work that I had prayed for and help the officers who are so special to me. How many people can say that? The job had not existed when I started writing this book.

I can reflect over the years I've spent in so many different aspects of the job, and I am overwhelmed at how God has transformed me throughout the process.

I started this job as a rookie, confident in my

own ability. I saw the ugliest side of society and blamed the people in it for the darkness. I lost one son and continue to watch my other son battle with drug addiction. I have experienced the deterioration of two marriages and have grappled with my own battle with cancer.

It took time and a lot of persistence on His part, but God eventually broke through the walls of my heart and opened me up to a relationship with Him. Through Him, I experienced comfort after my son T.T.'s death and throughout my other son's treatments. He also gave me peace while I went through my own cancer treatments.

As I mentioned, one of my prayers is that I be one with Jesus. John 15:4 says, *"Remain in me, as I also remain in you. No branch can bear fruit by itself; it must remain in the vine. Neither can you bear fruit unless you remain in me."* When we do that, the things we used to take pleasure in are not interesting anymore, and our hearts become one with Him.

God only wants the best for us, and He knows that involves being in constant relationship with Him.

When I began "abiding in the vine," God changed my entire outlook on life, but despite that, I felt true joy eluded me, until now. After beating cancer, I have a new outlook on life. I wake up in the morning, and I am genuinely happy to be alive.

Shortly before I was set to go back to work, I was asked to speak at a large conference for fellow law enforcement and other safety personnel. I was among a number of speakers, most of whom had national notoriety for their experiences. I couldn't help but feel under-qualified to be listed on the agenda alongside many of them.

But I prayed that God would use me however He needed to. Even hours before I was scheduled to take the podium, I was unsure about what I would say. I wasn't sure whether I should speak boldly about my faith or be more subtle as I knew there would be many in the audience who might not be receptive to God.

But as He had before, God gave me the words just in time. I shared my testimony, the loss of my son, and what God has done in my life. During a break in the conference, a number of people approached me and told me how they were affected by my story.

I don't want to sound like one of the "happy clappy" people, but I can't help but express my utter joy and appreciation for this life that God has given me. This exact life—including the grief and hardship, the pain and the struggles.

CHAPTER SIXTEEN
DEATH'S STING DEFEATED

I CORINTHIANS 15:55-58

"Where, O death, is your victory?
Where, O death, is your sting?"
The sting of death is sin, and the power of sin is the law.
But thanks be to God! He gives us the victory
through our Lord Jesus Christ.

SHE WAS RAISED FROM THE DEAD TO SAY GOODBYE

One day I was visiting a prayer chapel when I overheard a couple talking about resurrection. They were discussing the miraculous act of raising a person from the dead. I thought their conversation was a little strange, but I didn't give it much thought. In the days and weeks following, God began to put the subject on my heart. I felt as though he was telling me I'd be involved in a resurrection somehow. Again, I thought to myself, "That is weird."

Honestly, I didn't think it made any sense, but I continued to pray for God to reveal Himself to me.

Because of my ranking as a patrol sergeant at that time, I was required to respond to calls involving the deceased. Department protocol requires a supervisor to look over the scene to make sure there are no suspicious circumstances.

About two months after my experience at the prayer chapel, we got a call of a suicidal woman. When officers arrived, they discovered a young woman in her early 20s hanging from the rafters in her garage. They cut her down and laid her in the driveway. Paramedics attempted to revive her, but she had no pulse. She was dead.

I responded to the scene, and by the time I arrived, the woman had been dead for about 20 minutes. I remember her face. It was blue, and her eyes were open, fixed and dilated. I have seen several people who were not breathing and had a chance of resuscitation, but this young woman was not one of them. I was standing over her when I heard God say to me, "This one. Pray over this one." As crazy as it seemed, I obeyed. I began to pray.

In cases like this, I depend on the Holy Spirit to lead my prayers. I wouldn't know what to pray for otherwise. This was definitely way out of my comfort zone. But I remember feeling the presence of the Holy Spirit, and at the same time, I felt the presence of a spiritual battle.

I recognized the spirit of death. I began to pray to bind the evil spirits as I prayed for the woman's revival. At one point, I reached down and touched her foot as I continued to pray. About ten minutes into my prayer, the woman slowly closed her eyes and then suddenly, one of the paramedics jumped back away from her and yelled, "She's got a pulse!" Then another paramedic yelled, "She's got a blood pressure!" The paramedics and firefighters seemed shocked. I then realized that the same Holy Spirit that had resurrected Jesus had just resurrected the young woman I was praying for, and I yelled, "Praise God!" as the emergency workers looked at me with bewilderment in their faces. They quickly loaded her up into an ambulance and rushed her to the hospital.

I contacted the young woman's mother to let her know that her daughter was being rushed to the hospital. I didn't share the fact that her daughter had been dead, but I told her I had been praying for her and assured her that God was with the family. The young woman lived a few days, but she passed away in the hospital.

I know God was doing something special with that situation. I believe that those few days she remained alive were a gift to her family. Her mother got the chance to touch her daughter's warm hand and say goodbye.

Revelations 19:10 (NLT) says, *"The essence of prophecy is to give a clear witness for Jesus."* I believe the resurrection did just that. It strengthened my faith and brought glory to God. Two of my colleagues had been standing by watching the whole thing.

I learned later the effect it had on them. For days following the event, they continued to talk about what happened, and the discussion often turned to Jesus. For me, the event was symbolic. On so many levels, death has lost its sting. I know that it may be difficult for many people to believe in a modern-day resurrection. I never would have believed it when my story began, but that is where faith comes in. A huge part of my transformation involved the level of my faith.

I went from a man of no faith to one with the faith of a mustard seed. When I began to pray for more faith, God gave it to me, along with all the supernatural and wonderful blessings only He can provide.

A LITTLE GIRL NOW CANCER-FREE; NOTHING IS IMPOSSIBLE, FAITH CAN MOVE MOUNTAINS

I am also continually encouraged by the ongoing testimonies of God's impact on the lives of others. I was presented the opportunity to counsel another father whose two-year-old daughter had been diagnosed with cancer. She'd developed tumors throughout her body, and her prognosis wasn't good. Having been in the same shoes, my heart became heavy as I imagined this father traveling the same journey I had experienced with my son. I asked the father if I could say a prayer over his daughter, and he unexpectedly agreed. We prayed for his daughter's healing and for peace for him and his family. Shortly after, this man and his family headed up to a hospital in Northern California where his daughter was expected to receive treatment. However, when they got there, they received some unexpected news instead. The little girl was cured!

Doctors said it was miraculous. She was free of her cancer! Everything the doctors had seen before was now completely gone! The girl's father sent me an email with the news. All I can say is, "Hallelujah! Praise God!" He is so good. I have only recently opened up to the idea of healing prayers. I had been skeptical of them before because I'd received so many for my son T.T. But I now realize that God is so much bigger than I could ever fathom, and He can do anything.

After I'd given my life to Christ, I had a hard time believing in the power of healing prayers, but then I received it. I continued to doubt such prayers, but God continued to show me nothing is impossible through Him. Now, I have the faith to pray for healing—even from death. If we don't have faith that things are going to happen, they aren't going to happen. On the flip side, if we continue to pray for it, God will provide it. The best part is, He wants us all to have the kind of faith that moves mountains.

The first step is simply accepting Jesus Christ as Savior. We don't have to be slaves to our sins. We just have to claim victory by simply laying them down at the cross. The Gospel is so simple. Because of sin, no one is worthy of having a relationship with God. Not one of us. But because He loves us so much, He was willing to send His only son to die a horrific death on earth to atone for our sinful nature. The significance of that kind of sacrifice is not lost on most parents, including myself. All God asks of us is that we accept that grace.

Romans 10:9 says, *"If you declare with your mouth, 'Jesus is Lord,' and believe in your heart that God raised him from the dead, you will be saved."*

As simple as it is, many people find it tough to do. All I can do is share my experiences and pray that God might use my life to reach someone who hadn't been willing to listen before.

My faith is not the only thing that has transformed throughout my journey. My metamorphosis began when I went from simply being a sinner to becoming a new creation in Christ. It continued as I realized that the direction I was going in on my own continually lead to dead-ends. I then aligned my steps with the Lord. Just like Psalm 119:105 (KJV) says, *"Thy word is a lamp unto my feet and a light unto my path."*

He has shown me a very clear direction and path for my life that involves the care, and in many cases, the salvation of my fellow cops, first responders, and members of our military.

Finally, that hope for my future has brought me a level of fulfillment I never knew before. It has also provided me with excitement and great anticipation of things to come. Before, I would have let the cancer drag me down.

Of course, I'd rather not experience physical pain and discomfort, but I am certain God allowed me to endure it so it could become one more tool in my spiritual arsenal. The illness opened doors for me to minister to people in the hospital. Having gone through chemo, I can sit down with somebody who is suffering and tell them, "I get it."

Now, I only see God's blessings. The world wants us to see things through worldly eyes, but God is just waiting for us to tap into His kingdom. When we do, He is waiting to pour His blessings out on us.

I see it in my daily life, and I know I have barely scratched the surface.

In the case of my son, T.T., I know he's in a better place. He's with the Lord, and I know I will see him again. The Bible talks about Heaven often. One of my favorite passages is in Isaiah. We are told there will be no tears in Heaven, and the lame will leap like deer. That gives me so much comfort. I know that T.T. has two legs—or whatever it is we get when we get to Heaven!

As for my 187 tattoo, I now repent for the bloodletting and self-harm I committed and for the agreement I made with that spirit. I claim I Corinthians 15:55-58 over my life and my family's lives, in Jesus' name.

The verse says:

"Where, O death, is your victory?
Where, O death, is your sting?"
The sting of death is sin, and the power of sin is the law. But thanks be to God! He gives us the victory through our Lord Jesus Christ.
Therefore, my dear brothers and sisters, stand firm. Let nothing move you. Always give yourselves fully to the work of the Lord, because you know that your labor in the Lord is not in vain.

My prayer is that my story will have a real impact on anyone who opens this book, whether it's the first time hearing the Gospel, or whether they've sat in church a hundred Sundays and have simply lost sight of God's purpose for their life.

I know that God can use anyone who is obedient and willing to listen. Over the years, I've learned to be, and continue to strive to be, open to God's plans. It is about stepping out and walking in faith, whether that means praying with a driver during a traffic stop or a family member who's lost a loved one or a convicted killer in a hospital bed.

SET THE CAPTIVES FREE; JESUS OFFERS FREEDOM

For the first time in my life, I recently had the humbling experience of leading someone else to the

Lord. My best friend Matt's niece had been arrested for a drug-related offense. When I heard about her situation, I immediately reached out to her mother (Matt's sister) to ask if there was anything I could do to help. Her mother asked if I'd be willing to simply go down to the jail and talk to her daughter.

We met in a dim, dirty, and dank room where we were able to visit. I think it was symbolic of the nature of the young girl's heart at that point. She had been struggling with addiction, and she was very aware of how her arrest had embarrassed and affected her family. She was a victim of the enemy, who wants to attack us with shame and keep us from the forgiveness and freedom of a relationship with Jesus.

As we talked, I shared with her what Jesus had to offer and told her she did not need to continue to carry around the burdens that were dragging her down. She told me she was ready to accept Jesus as her Savior, and I led her through confession and a prayer for salvation, right there in that grimy jail.

Again, that is the beauty of God's grace. He deeply desires a relationship with us, despite our deepest flaws.

After I left the jail, I reached out to the girl's mother a few days later, and she told me the testimony that her daughter had relayed about receiving Christ in jail. I believe that this testimony has released a prophetic word that will allow God's grace to work in a powerful way in this entire family, a family which I love and care for in a very special way. I also know that there is a great deal of hope for this young woman in the future.

I began to reflect on the girl's grandfather, Matt's

dad, who'd passed away from cancer when we were just adolescents. He had never had the opportunity to meet his granddaughter, but God used him to impact me more than a decade before she was even born. The grandfather's faith brought peace and strength to his family during his death and touched me and stayed with me. Now I can see that the strength he exhibited during his fight with cancer was simply the peace he received from his walk with the Lord. That small seed that he planted in me took years to grow, but I believe that it's partly because of his example that I ended up in the position to witness to his granddaughter, whom he had never met.

God is real. He speaks to us if we are willing to listen and obey. I encourage people to be courageous and use the spiritual gifts that God has given them. We can glorify Him simply by speaking boldly of Jesus, for everything comes from Him and exists by His power and is intended for His glory. Amen.

ACKNOWLEDGMENTS

LUKE 1:37

"For no word from God will ever fail."

FIRST AND FOREMOST, we want to thank God. We prayed for His guidance, and He was always faithful to provide us with inspiration, insight, and grace. When we needed help, He provided us with people who could offer it. When we needed encouragement, He supplied it in abundance. With Him, all things are possible.

This book was truly a group effort. We could not have completed it without a number of very talented, kind and generous supporters. We want to recognize all of the people who made this project a reality. Michael Hammer, for your dedication and encouragement; John Johnson, for your expertise and unwavering optimism; Chuk Reed, for your wisdom and for allowing us to share a small part of your own incredible story. Also, George Armstrong, Jay Carty, Michael Bayouth, Lacy Reynolds, Dean Wilder, and everyone at DP Consulting for providing us with much-needed guidance.

Finally, we thank our families for offering support and encouragement along the journey. We cannot express the depth of our gratitude. Thank you.

ABOUT THE AUTHOR

SARA BUSH is a seasoned journalist who has covered numerous major events in the Southern California region as both a television news reporter and newspaper journalist. Her proven reputation as a bold and accurate journalist drew the attention of Sergeant Mike McGrew while she reported many of the major crimes he responded to and investigated during his career.

The editor of the local newspaper asked Sara to write a story about Sgt. McGrew, following his cancer diagnosis. As Sara interviewed Sgt. McGrew for the article, he shared with her his testimony of faith. The story made the front page of the paper.

Sgt. McGrew felt the article captured accurately what God had done in his life and admired the boldness of the author, speaking the name of Jesus in the front-page article. It was because of Sara Bush's skills as a writer and her personal integrity that Sgt. McGrew felt led to recruit Sara Bush to help him write his memoir.

While Sara Bush had always planned on becoming an author, the path leading to this project could only be described as divine intervention. Writing this book changed the course of Sara's life. As Sgt. McGrew puts it, "The story behind this book is a story in itself."

In addition to author and journalist, Sara is a wife and mother of two beautiful children.